THE
TIMES OF
A GIFT

BRYAN MEADOWS

The Times of a Gift
Bryan Meadows

© 2021, Bryan Meadows
www.bryanmeadows.com
bryan@embassychurchatl.com

Published by Embassy Advantage™

Cover Design by Justin Foster

Diagrams by Picture It Possible

Editing and Research Team:
Tiffany Buckner
Georgie-Ann Neil

ISBN: 978-1-7348612-6-6

Table of Contents

Introduction

This is the book for the creative and the gift who wants to understand time and how it affects us and our giftings! This is the book for the emerging gifts of tomorrow who want to avoid the copious snares that many of the gifts who've gone before them have fallen into!

In this monumental and enlightening guide, you will get the language you need for the season you're in, the seasons you've been through and the seasons you're about to enter! You will not only get the language for these seasons, but you will learn how to master each season so that you can extract its benefits and break through to the next season! *The Times of a Gift* is a smorgasbord of revelation and information that will prove to be both beneficial and empowering! This amazing book will prove to be a potent and much-needed tool in the creative's arsenal!

You are empowered to win, but perverted to fail! You need a Joshua to hold up your arms when you grow weary, and this powerful and delightful guide will prove to be just that! *The Times of a Gift* will teach you how to penetrate the defenses of the enemy so that you can arrive in a place called purpose! Take a journey with me through history, science and revelation, and I can assure you that after reading this dynamic guide, your life and your journey will never look the same again!

The World of Gifts

Gift: "something given to someone without expectation of a return" (Merriam-Webster).

Synonyms for Gift			
allowance	offering	bequest	handout
award	premium	bestowal	honorarium
benefit	present	boon	lagniappe
bonus	relief	bounty	largesse
contribution	reward	charity	libation
donation	souvenir	courtesy	oblation
endowment	subsidy	dispensation	offertory
favor	tip	fairing	philanthropy
giveaway	tribute	gratuity	pittance
grant	alms	hand	presentation
legacy	benefaction	hand-me-down	handout
Ration	Remembrance	Remittance	Subscription
Token	Write-off	Goodie	Provision

Source: Thesaurus.com/Gift

First, let's talk about the different types of gifts, which are:
- Natural Gifts
- Spiritual Gifts
- Gifts of the Spirit

Natural Gifts

In short, natural gifts are talents or abilities that are oftentimes passed down to us from our parents. When most people talk about purpose, they typically associate this with their natural gifts. For example, you'll notice that in some families, just about everyone can sing. In some families, you'll notice that a lot of the members are skilled at creating things like clothes, jewelry, pottery or so on. The members of each family seem to be born with an innate ability to do a thing and to do it well.

The purpose of a natural gift is to help you develop your character and earn money. This is done through repetition. You have to repeatedly do a thing before you can master it. Malcolm Gladwell, the renowned and bestselling author of the book Outliers, says in his book, "To become an expert, it takes 10000 hours (or approximately ten years) of deliberate practice." Many critics have arisen to debunk this theory, but it has some air of truth to it. You can't expect to be the best in a specific field after a single year of working in that field. Be sure to read the parable of the talents found in Matthew 25:14-30. In this, each man had been given a unique ability. One man had five unique abilities, another man had two unique abilities and another guy had a single unique ability. The one who had five went and doubled his abilities. The one who had two went and increased in his abilities. But the guy who had one ability was a sluggard. He buried his ability in the ground. Please note that when the scriptures refer to dirt or ground, this is symbolic of flesh. He was a lazy man who was full of excuses. So, God took away his unique ability, and consequently, a generational curse was born, whereas, his children and their children would not have any unique abilities. This means that they had to work for those who were talented. The man who had five unique abilities increased in wisdom and wealth, and when the master (a type and shadow of Jesus) came back and saw that he'd been faithful, he'd been diligent and he'd been consistent, He said to the man, "I will make you a ruler of many things. Enter now into the joy of the Lord." Statistics have proven that wealthy people stay married longer, live longer and are better off physically. This is joy; that is, of course, for the ones who earned their wealth the right way. And please note that the Greek word for "joy" is "chara," and it literally means "gladness, delight or rejoicing."

Spiritual Gifts

Spiritual gifts are often confused with gifts of the spirit. These are gifts or talents that we cannot track or trace. They are similar to talents, however, they are not genetic. A perfect example would be David's ability as a minstrel. The Bible doesn't say that his father, Jesse, had been a minstrel. Jesse was a farmer and a shepherd. The same was true for David. He inherited that particular skill and ability, but his ability to sing and play the lyre is untraceable. However, we do see these gifts showing up in his son, Solomon, since Solomon was also a psalmist.

Gifts of the Spirit		
Word of Knowledge	Word of Wisdom	Gift of Prophecy
Gift of Faith	Discerning of Spirits	Gifts of Healing
Working of Miracles	Speaking in Tongues	Interpretation of Tongues

1 Corinthians 12:4-11: Now there are diversities of gifts, but the same Spirit. And there are differences of administrations, but the same Lord. And there are diversities of operations, but it is the same God which worketh all in all. But the manifestation of the Spirit is given to every man to profit withal. For to one is given by the Spirit the word of wisdom; to another the word of knowledge by the same Spirit; to another faith by the same Spirit; to another the gifts of healing by the same Spirit; To another the working of miracles; to another prophecy; to another discerning of spirits; to another divers kinds of tongues; to another the interpretation of tongues: But all these worketh that one and the selfsame Spirit, dividing to every man severally as he will.

Gifts of the Spirit are supernatural abilities given to believers through the power of the Holy Spirit for the purpose of building and growing the church.

- **Word of Knowledge:** This is the ability to know information that was not shared with you. This is similar to the gift of prophecy, howbeit, prophecy deals with the future, but words of knowledge usually reference the past and the present.

4

- **Word of Wisdom:** Knowledge is information that has been shared with you, but wisdom is supernatural knowledge coupled with understanding that produces faith. This is what the Bible refers to as a word spoken in due season (see Proverbs 15:23).
- **Gift of Prophecy:** This is the ability to hear God and communicate with others what's on the heart of God. Prophecies are also associated with futuristic events, instructions and warnings.
- **Gift of Faith:** According to the scriptures, every believer should have a measure of faith, but there are levels of faith. Jesus spoke of the great faith of the centurion who believed that He could heal his servant without touching him (see Matthew 8:5-13). He spoke of little faith when calming His disciples after they'd panicked and awakened Him during a storm (see Matthew 8:26). The Bible says that Abraham had "strong faith" because he didn't stagger regarding the promises of God (see Romans 4:20). The gift of faith is a supernatural measure of faith given to men like Moses, Noah and Apostle Paul that allows them to believe God beyond their understanding.
- **Discerning of Spirits:** This is the supernatural ability to know when someone is in need of deliverance and to know the types of spirits that you are encountering. You will find this gift in deliverance ministers, not to be confused with people who've simply learned how to cast out devils. Deliverance ministers are a unique group of gifts who are emboldened with knowledge of

5

the spirit realm and the courage to confront unclean spirits, as well as identify them.

- **Gifts of Healing:** This is another gift of faith that allows some believers to lay hands on the sick and heal them through the power of the Holy Spirit. Again, healing is a gift that every believer is empowered with, but there are some people who are graced for this specific area of ministry. Because of this, they can see and eradicate illnesses, deformations and disorders in the body.

- **Working of Miracles:** We saw this gift in action when Moses went before Pharaoh on multiple occasions. We also witnessed this particular grace when Jesus turned water into wine and when the widow's jar of flour and jug of oil kept supernaturally refilling themselves after she'd followed Elijah's instructions.

- **Speaking in Tongues:** This means to speak in a Heavenly language. This gift allows the believer to surpass his or her own understanding to speak directly to God. This also grows the faith of the believer, especially when someone is present to give each believer utterance.

- **Interpretation of Tongues:** This is the supernatural and wonderful ability to interpret a language that is Heavenly. When a believer speaks in tongues, he or she doesn't understand what he or she is saying because the language the believer is using is not of this world. In order for someone to interpret tongues, the Holy Spirit has to give that person utterance.

Understanding Your Gifts

Turn on your television and just flip through the channels. What you are seeing is a buffet of gifts. But first, what exactly is a gift? Merriam-Webster defines the word "gift" as "something voluntarily transferred by one person to another without compensation." Let's look at some of the gifts that God gave us.

- **1 Corinthians 12:4-11:** Now there are diversities of gifts, but the same Spirit. And there are differences of administrations, but the same Lord. And there are diversities of operations, but it is the same God which worketh all in all. But the manifestation of the Spirit is given to every man to profit withal. For to one is given by the Spirit the word of wisdom; to another the word of knowledge by the same Spirit; to another faith by the same Spirit; to another the gifts of healing by the same Spirit; to another the working of miracles; to another prophecy; to another discerning of spirits; to another divers kinds of tongues; to another the interpretation of tongues: But all these worketh that one and the selfsame Spirit, dividing to every man severally as he will.

- **Ephesians 4:8-12:** Wherefore he saith, When he ascended up on high, he led captivity captive, and gave gifts unto men. (Now that he ascended, what is it but that he also descended first into the lower parts of the earth? He that descended is the same also that ascended up far above all heavens, that he might fill all things.) And he gave some, apostles; and some,

7

prophets; and some, evangelists; and some, pastors and teachers; for the perfecting of the saints, for the work of the ministry, for the edifying of the body of Christ.

- **John 3:16:** or God so loved the world, that he gave his only begotten Son, that whosoever believeth in him should not perish, but have everlasting life.
- **John 20:22:** And when he had said this, he breathed on them, and saith unto them, Receive ye the Holy Ghost.

This is just a short list of what God has given us, with the most important of these gifts being Jesus and the Holy Spirit. There are gifts in Heaven and gifts on Earth. Revelation 2:4-11 reads, "And immediately I was in the spirit: and, behold, a throne was set in heaven, and one sat on the throne. And he that sat was to look upon like a jasper and a sardine stone: and there was a rainbow round about the throne, in sight like unto an emerald. And round about the throne were four and twenty seats: and upon the seats I saw four and twenty elders sitting, clothed in white raiment; and they had on their heads crowns of gold. And out of the throne proceeded lightnings and thunderings and voices: and there were seven lamps of fire burning before the throne, which are the seven Spirits of God. And before the throne there was a sea of glass like unto crystal: and in the midst of the throne, and round about the throne, were four beasts full of eyes before and behind. And the first beast was like a lion, and the second beast like a calf, and the third beast had a face as a man, and the fourth beast was like a flying eagle. And the four beasts had each of them six wings about him; and they were full of eyes within: and they rest not day and night, saying, Holy, holy, holy, Lord God Almighty, which was, and is, and is to come. And when those beasts give glory and honour and thanks to him that sat on the throne, who liveth for ever and ever, The four and twenty elders fall down before him that sat on the throne, and worship him that liveth for ever and ever, and cast their crowns before the throne, saying, Thou art worthy, O Lord, to receive glory and honour and power: for thou hast created all things, and for thy pleasure they are and were created." This is to bring to your attention that there are different types of creatures (gifts) in Heaven, and the way each creature is designed is directly related to that creature's functions or assignments. God's will is done on Earth as it is in Heaven. Also note that the Greek word for "gift" is "charisma" and it literally means "grace" or "undeserved favor."

Gift	Gifted	Gifted

These are three words that we must understand before we proceed any further. Let's define the three.
- **Gift:** This is the ability or the talent to do a thing.
- **Gifted:** This deals with education. This is when you take your ability to a level of competence through training, education, development or mentorship.
- **Gifting:** This is the unique fingerprint of your specific gift. It's when you start to find the nuance of your

authenticity.

Michael Jackson had a gift. He could sing and dance. He was gifted, meaning he mastered his abilities by studying people like Jackie Wilson and James Brown. He then moved over into gifting by taking what he'd learned and combining it with his own personality and his own skills and abilities, thus, creating his own unique expression. This is when his nuances merge with his skill and ability to make them distinct. Gifting is the thing that you can do that nobody else can do. It's what makes that specific gift your own. For example, Michael Jordan, Tiger Woods and Will Smith all are in industries that are well populated with gifts, but these men have taken those industries by storm by not only mastering their crafts but by making them their own. All the same, the moment you give your abilities to a specific industry and that industry is able to benefit from your abilities, you then become a gift. Jesus was gifted, but He was also a gift to mankind. Likewise, the apostle, prophet, pastor, evangelist and teacher are all gifts to the church.

One of the movies I think most of us enjoyed when we were young was *Willy Wonka and the Chocolate Factory*. This is because this movie depicted a world that, for a child, is almost utopic. Waterfalls made entirely of chocolate, gardens made of candy, giant lollipops and musicals; it's a movie that brings some of a child's greatest fantasies to life. And if we're honest, we love movies, especially the ones that depict realities that don't mirror the ones that we live in because they provide us with a way to mentally escape our own worlds. They take us into the imaginations of other people, and we get to experience, albeit vicariously, what it would be like to live outside of what we've come to know as "normal." We all want to experience paradise, and this may not look the same for all of us. This is why there are different genres of movies, all of which appeal to a certain crowd. This is also why we are so attracted to the idea of Heaven. We imagine streets paved with gold, resting on plush clouds, surrounded by waterfalls and everything that we consider to be lovely. We imagine Heaven being a place where all of our needs are met and our fantasies are fulfilled. This is because, to us, Heaven represents another world. It's almost like another planet; it is an escape from the world we know. And what makes it so exciting is that Heaven is forever. But rarely do we think outside of ourselves when thinking about paradise. In truth, we need to understand that Heaven isn't a place where we'll get to be eternally selfish, we will still have responsibilities; we will all be worshiping God in our own unique ways. This is why we all have gifts. For example, Willy Wonka had workers called Oompa-Loompas. Willy Wonka had a total of 165 Oompa-Loompas working for him. Their job was to run the factory. This means that the factory was a world within itself, meaning it had a system in place. What we have to understand about a system is that it is a series of unique parts that are all interconnected. If one of these parts stop moving, the entire system can stall and the machine can malfunction. The same is true in the world of gifts. When one individual doesn't do what he or she is designed to do, this creates a domino effect. In truth, it starts another system. How so? Chances are, his children will follow in his footsteps. This also means that something that should have been created or done in the Earth is not completed. This leaves what we call a void. According to Oxford Languages, the word "void" means "a completely empty space." Think about your favorite fast food restaurant. If the cooks were to suddenly call out one day, this would stall their system and cause people who were supposed to be functioning at the registers and in the windows to have to go into the kitchen. This means that they'll be short-staffed. Of course, they'd likely attempt to call some people in who are off that day, but most people won't answer their phones when they see their employers calling them on their days off. So, if you and I were to pull up to that particular restaurant, what we'd find are long lines and a bunch of frustrated workers. The girl who is great at customer service may be in the back cooking. The girl who normally busses tables may be working the register, and she simply does not have the patience to work with people. The guy working the window normally works the register, and while he's okay with working the window, his pace does not match his position. This means that when a person does not use his or her gifting, a void in the Earth is not filled, and people called to other industries have to be misplaced in order to fill those voids. Needless to say, our Earth is filled with voids right now because we have a lot of gifted people who are not where they should be.

Systems and Processes

There are many worlds in this planet, but before we come to understand this, we must first understand that the word "world" does not reference planets. It means system. A planet can be a part of a system, for example, there is a planetary system. There are many worlds on Earth, including our ecosystem, our hydrosphere, our prison systems, the systems of our body; it's all broad and without ends. Everything that exists, functions and reproduces itself in any capacity is a part of a system. Oxford Languages defines the word "system" as "a set of things working together as parts of a mechanism or an interconnecting network." Romans 8:28 states, "And we know that all things work together for good to them that love God, to them who are the called according to his purpose." Of course, Romans 8:28 is referencing Kingdom systems. Your body is a system, and within it, there are many sub-systems. The food industry is a system, and within it, there are many sub-systems which include grocery stores, farmers' markets, restaurants, and so on. There is a world of finances, a world of health, a world of beauty, a world of science, and the list is endless. These are all systems that are held together or interconnected by a series of sub-systems. This means that every one of these is a world within itself. Then again, we have a world of gifts or gifted people, and like every other system, it is a broad world that stretches to the ends of the Earth and is broken up into many sub-systems. And these gifts (creatives) have been sprinkled into just about every system on the face of this planet where they are required to use their gifts. Let's consider the Seven Mountains of Influence, which are the mountains of:

- Family
- Media
- Arts and Entertainment
- Religion
- Government
- Education
- Business

All of these worlds are populated with gifts; there are low-ranking gifts and there are high-ranking gifts. In the world or system of media, you will find social media, television, music, radio and many other forms of communication. Social media has many sub-systems, including Facebook, Twitter, Instagram, YouTube, Linkedin and the list keeps growing. On Facebook, there are many sides or dimensions. There is the Christian side, there is a side completely dedicated to video games, there is an occultic side, etc. And while there is no specific page to navigate to in order to enter each world, there are pages and groups created for people with like interests. If I were to go and send friend requests to a bunch of satanists, Facebook's algorithm would kick in and Facebook would recommend more satanists for me to befriend. The point is, there are many systems, sub-systems, groups and sub-groups on this planet; there are many worlds that make up this planet, and we are all called to one or more of these systems. Your gift only reaches its full potential in certain worlds. A fish doesn't live above water; it was built to survive and thrive underwater. All the same, a professional swimmer's gift is useless on a mountain; that is unless the swimmer finds a body of water deep enough to jump into. A singer's gift is pointless in a room filled with deaf people. This doesn't stop the singer from being a singer; this doesn't stop the singer from being gifted! The problem is the people around her can't hear her, so her gift, while it may be powerful, while it may be needed and while it may be sharpened, has no value or use in specific worlds. A sprinter's gift is useless in water, a hairstylist's gift is pointless in a room filled with bald people and a chef's gift is useless in a room filled with newborn babies. This means that there is a time for a gift and a gift for a time. It also means that there is a space on Earth cut out for your anointing, your gifting and whatever specific set of skills you have.

When discussing the Seven Mountains of Influence, we have to take the concept of a natural mountain into consideration. Without being too expansive, there are levels and sides to every mountain, and not every hiker will reach the peak of every mountain. All the same, hikers don't normally ascend every side of a mountain. In other words, not every gift will have the same measure of influence, after all, influence is God's trust. Some gifts will remain at the bottom of the mountain, but hear me—they are just as important as the men and women who are called to the top. This has to be emphasized in this day and age because a lot of believers are overly determined to become celebrities, not realizing

15

that on every level of the mountains that we ascend, there is a certain amount of pressure. These pressures are called winds, and if we don't have enough substance or our character doesn't have enough weight to resist the winds (temptations), we will bow down to the many pressures that come on each level and we will become just another fallen gift. Spiritually speaking, the Mountains of Influence are littered with the carcasses of gifts. The carcass of a gift is called potential.

You are a gift, and as such, you belong to a specific world. Sure, you may have close friends who belong to other worlds, and it is common (and normal) for gifts when they are in the puberty of their giftings to want to congregate around the people who share similar interests as you. You can have similar interests and plans with people from many worlds, but it does not mean that you're called to the same mountains, the same sides of a mountain or the same levels of a mountain (measure of influence). Then again, you may be called to several industries; this is also common. But there is a season or a time for every world, and if you enter that world prematurely, you can easily forfeit your destiny.

Missing Gifts

In the 70's, 80's and 90's, it was common to find the faces of missing children on the front of milk cartons. The reason lawmakers took this route was because those same milk cartons were being distributed to just about every school in the United States. This would ensure that every child had the opportunity to look at the face of a missing child and see if he or she recognized that child. This was an ingenious tactic, and it actually produced a lot of happy endings! But did you know that in the world of gifts, there are many missing gifts who simply have not arrived to the height of their potential? Physically, they can be found, but they cannot be found in purpose. This is because they are following someone or something else around in another world, hoping to find or create a place for themselves in that world or make a name for themselves in that world. One of my assignments (in life and in this book) is to help people to get comfortable with the world or system that they're called to! But before I can do this, I have to help them to accept the fact that there are many worlds on this planet, and we are not called to all of them. This is why we have so many insecure or timid gifts! They are gifted people who are trying to introduce their gifts to the wrong people or the wrong industries! And before we delve deeper into this lesson, let's talk about three enemies or unclean spirits that will try to seduce you outside of the world that you're called to. They are:

1. Envy
2. Mammon
3. Trauma

Envy

Envy is a seducer. It understands that you are called to a specific industry or world, a specific group of people, a specific amount of people and a specific type of people. And by type, I'm talking about people with a unique set of interests. In the world of business, this is referred to as your "target audience." Your gift works best in the correct industry or on the right mountain. If you are called to the mountain of government but are operating in the mountain of arts and media, you will still remain gifted, but the problem is, you're in the wrong system or world. This means that you are an alien in that world or a foreigner to that world, and while you may produce many things, they won't amount to much because what you will have to do to sustain yourself in that world is exchange your gifting for a skill-set. What's amazing is, many people flourish off their skills. They make a lot of money and find their versions of success while tapping into a skill-set that they've learned. But if you were to speak with most of these people, you'd find that they are miserable, tired and frustrated. They're always being tormented by the demons of comparison and fear, and they are always worried about their businesses or whatever it is that they've built. This is what Envy did to them. It seduced them outside the will of God into a place where their gifts would be of little to no value. It then began to attack their mental health. We must understand that Satan is present in every system except the Kingdom of God. This means that every gift must remain prayerful and every gift must remain within the confines of God's will; this is how the creative remains protected from the many snares that have been set against him or her.

Mammon

This has to be the number one seducer for God's gifts! And

it's not money that's an issue, it's the love of money or the need for money. This gives birth to fear and impatience, and it effectively causes many gifts to squander their potential every day! The spirit of impatience is a bullying spirit that launches a bunch of timed and calculated attacks against believers. What this devil does is, highlights and magnifies a set of problems in the believer's life. For example, Billy needs money and he needs it fast! His rent is past due, his electric bill has doubled and his car is scheduled to be repossessed any day now! But Billy is anointed, he is gifted and he is called to the mountain of government. Nevertheless, Billy needs money and he needs it now! And even though he's in school studying Political Science, he's skilled at making glass objects. It is a skill he's acquired from his father who was a renowned glass maker before his untimely death. No college student is willing to pay Billy to make anything for him or her, so one day, Billy, in his desperation, found himself talking to a guy who he once avoided. Within that college, there are many children dabbling in drugs and James is a part of that particular world. And once he learns that Billy is skilled at creating glass objects, he immediately asks him, "Can you make a glass hookah?" Billy looks both confused and concerned, but James knows what to say to relax him. "Man, if you can make glass hookahs, I'm telling you, you will never have to worry about being broke!" That was it! Billy agrees to make a few hookahs for James, and before long, he is being contacted every day by students who want him to make hookahs for them. This brings in a lot of money, but that money begins to dwindle because, before long, just about every student in that particular world or system has already purchased one or more hookahs. Desperate, Billy listens to a suggestion made by another student who'd purchased a hookah from him. Nya said to Billy, "If you sold hookahs with the drugs already in them, you'd make a killing!" Billy? A drug dealer?! No, this seems too far-fetched, but desperation, greed and his budding love of money takes over, and before long, Billy finds himself selling drugs. Eventually, he is arrested and expelled from school. How would he make his way to the mountain of government now? This would definitely be an uphill journey! Again, many gifts forfeit their mountains when they are completely unaware of who they are, and they often do this because of their love for money. Of course, Mammon is the principality (ruling spirit) behind the love of money.

Trauma

If trauma were a drug, we'd all be addicts or recovering addicts on the verge of relapsing! Out of all the weapons he's ever manufactured, trauma is one of Satan's most potent weapons! I immediately think about Oprah. She'd suffered many traumas growing up, one of them being sexual abuse. According to Oprah, she was raped by one of her older cousins. This is a crime that happens in the dark. It silences the victim and teaches him or her to master keeping secrets. Victims of sexual abuse are oftentimes afraid of spotlights because their attackers are skilled at making them feel like they were complicit in their own attacks. This opens the door for guilt and shame, and it causes the victims to shy away from anything and anyone that remotely threatens to expose what they believe to be their secrets. This is the complete opposite of what Oprah does today. She has a lot of exposure. She has to stand or sit in front of millions of people, talking about every hot topic that floods our airwaves, including her own life. You see, in order to connect with your audiences, you need to find common ground, so when Oprah opened up about her past, she attracted millions of people to her who had similar testimonies. Howbeit, trauma was and is designed to silence her, just as it is designed to silence you. Trauma not only silences people, but it also makes them want to speak out of turns. It partners with impatience and dishonor, and it causes many gifts to chase after spotlights and mics so that they can tell their stories. And while their stories should be heard, there is a season for them to be heard! All too often, they aren't healed enough to spotlight their pasts. They need counseling first. The reason for this is, trauma victims are oftentimes so angry and traumatized that they'll stop at nothing to see their attackers lynched, crucified, castrated, beheaded or destroyed. And this leads many people to discredit themselves by adding extra details to their stories in their attempts at ensuring that their offenders are prosecuted or punished. When these discrepancies are made known, it discredits the voice of the victim, and in many cases, silences the victim forever, causing them to be further victimized. This is why counseling is needed first.

The point is, there are many systems and worlds, and you are called to one or more of them. But there are many forces that will try to keep you outside of your purpose and outside the will of God; this way, you never fulfill whatever it is that you were designed to accomplish. It's okay to be mesmerized or attracted to other worlds, but if you want to thrive on this Earth, you have to respect the world that you're called to and the process that you must endure to get into and ascend in that particular world.

Your Area Code
In the world of gifts, you will find everyone from basketball players, minstrels, psalmists, dancers, politicians, surgeons, accountants, actors, producers of every sort, painters, hairstylists, fashion designers, interior designers, nail techs, architects, carpenters, cooks, landscapers, scientists, app designers, graphic designers and, of course, this list is nearly infinite. Everyone's field has its own unique area code. The area code of your particular skill-set is the Mountain of Influence you're called to, but the zip code of your gift is the specific side of that mountain you're called to. Your phone number, on the other hand, is your gifting. What have you done to make the gift your own? What makes you stand out from the rest? What this means is that while we have a plethora of talented people, we all have our own spaces.

Imagine that somehow, I was taken and tossed into the middle of a Lakers game against the Clippers. They've given me my own uniform, shoes and socks, and now, I'm in the middle of the game trying to blend in with the rest of my team. I'm not a basketball player. Like most African American men my age, I can play basketball, but I'm not a professional. Sure, I've learned a lot about the game from the sidelines, but I've never been on the court with professional basketball players, so first off, I'd feel intimidated. Secondly, I'm not a professional. Can I play the game? Yes. Does this make me a basketball player? No. This is not my area code; it's not what I'm called to. Now, I've taken acting classes, and in college, I majored in theater, so I could definitely blend into the game, but if someone were to throw the ball to me, that's when my inadequacies would show. This doesn't mean that I can't play basketball. It simply means that I've never had a bunch of professional players running towards me at one time, while being aired live on national television. The point is, just because you can do something doesn't mean that you should do it.

Envy, comparison and insecurity causes many creatives to forsake the mountains and systems they are called to. This causes them to become villains in other industries. The reason for this is because you cannot and will not ascend a mountain unless you're called to it. Every other way to ascend that mountain for you would be illegal. Going back to *Willy Wonka and the Chocolate Factory*, if you can remember, Willy Wonka had an antagonist by the name of Mr. Slugsworth. Let's pretend that these were real men. It would be obvious that Willy Wonka was in the industry that he was called to, howbeit, Mr. Slugsworth would represent someone who was on the wrong mountain attempting to make a name for himself, but because candy-making didn't come naturally to him, he had to lie and steal in order to get ahead. Here's a snippet of an article I found on Villains Wiki:

"In the book, Arthur Slugworth is one of Willy Wonka's rival chocolatiers. Slugworth, along with Wonka's other rivals Mr. Fickelgruber and Mr. Prodnose, sent in spies to steal the secret recipes to Wonka's treats for them.

Having obtained these, he began making candy balloons that a consumer blows up to incredible sizes, and then causes to burst before eating them, a plagiarized invention.

The work of Slugworth (along with the other rivals) came close to ruining Wonka's factory. Wonka was forced to close his factory and fire all of his workers. A few years later, Wonka's factory began working again (operated exclusively by Oompa-Loompas) and his work continued to dominate the candy industry, with no rival able to plagiarize his work because using the Oompa Loompa as his workers enables Wonka to operate his factory without regular employees and keeping it off-limits to the public, so none of the spies can infiltrate.

Slugworth is never heard from again, but it is stated that Slugworth, Prodnose, or Fickelgruber would each give their front teeth to enter Wonka's inventing room (a laboratory) for five minutes. It's presumed that

Slugworth, alongside Prodnose and Fickelgruber, may have continued their businesses, but as Willy Wonka stopped hiring human employees, it's likely they no longer were able to produce special treats like those of Wonka" (Source: Villains Wiki/Arthur Slugsworth).

Again, people who forsake their own industries often become villains in other industries because what comes naturally to others does not come naturally to them. This reminds me of Newton's Third Law of Motion. The following information was taken from the Physics Classroom:

"For every action, there is an equal and opposite reaction. The statement means that in every interaction, there is a pair of forces acting on the two interacting objects. The size of the forces on the first object equals the size of the force on the second object. The direction of the force on the first object is opposite to the direction of the force on the second object. Forces always come in pairs - equal and opposite action-reaction force pairs" (Physics Classroom/Newton's Third Law).

Did you read that in its entirety?! This law isn't just for the natural realm, it's true in the realm of the spirit as well! In layman's terms, for every action, there is a reaction called opposition! When you find good, you will find something to oppose it. We call it evil! There is light, and then, there is something to oppose that light, which is darkness. There is a force that's going to oppose everything that you do! This means that you should be gifted, meaning you should attach an education to your gift! Again, we do this through mentorship, training, development and study. All the same, make sure you are on the right mountain; this way, your anointing will partner with your talent and produce miracles. Then again, you can allow jealousy and comparison to cause you to go into a system or an industry that you are not cut out for. That's like putting ice in a microwave! You are uniquely designed to perform a certain function in a certain environment. When you find your place of purpose, you'll find your superpowers. Sure, the world of gifts is one that is without ends, and every gift is needed to run these worlds; this is how we bring Heaven to Earth. And even though we have gifts, we can only become gifts to the worlds we are called to.

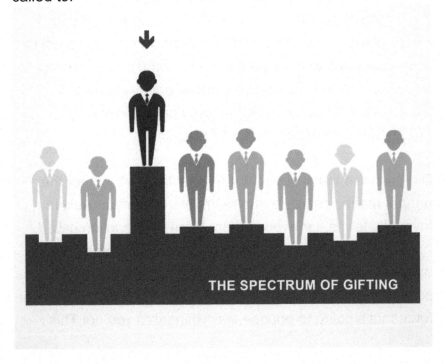

THE SPECTRUM OF GIFTING

Thy Kingdom Come

Before we break down the concept of time, let's discuss the word "forever" or the word "eternal." We have come to understand that, as spirits, we will live forever. This means that our souls and our spirits will be housed in eternity. The following definitions were taken from Oxford Languages:

- **Forever:** for all future time; for always.
- **Eternity:** infinite or unending time.
- **Eternal:** lasting or existing forever; without end or beginning.

The first two definitions are erroneous. How so? They encompass the words "time," but the definition for "eternal" is accurate because it says "without end or beginning." And as we very well know, God is eternal; He is the Beginning and the End, even though He has no beginning or end. This means that He exists outside of time. Anything that exists inside of the spectrum of time is limited since time is a space that houses both a beginning and an end. For example, the Earth was created in the beginning, and what we'll come to discover as we read this book is that the word "beginning" in Genesis 1 does not reference time. However, the moment the Earth was created was the beginning of the Earth. This means that the Earth's existence can be measured in Chronos time. The same is true for mankind. The moment Adam was created is called his beginning, just like the moment he died represented his end. Howbeit, Adam was and is a spirit, meaning that he did not cease to exist the moment he stopped breathing and his spirit left his body. Instead, his spirit transitioned into eternity, meaning he left the constructs or limitations of time where he now exists in eternity. The same is true for all human beings. We live inside the window of time, but once we leave our bodies, we will transition into eternity. This is because when God created man, He created him to live forever. Mankind, on the other hand, is a different breed of creature than man. Let's look at a few scriptures. Genesis 1:26-27 reads, "And God said, Let us make man in our image, after our likeness: and let them have dominion over the fish of the sea, and over the fowl of the air, and over the cattle, and over all the earth, and over every creeping thing that creepeth upon the earth. So God created man in his own image, in the image of God created he him; male and female created he them."

First and foremost, who was God speaking to when He said, "Let us make man in our image?" God exists in three persons; they are God (YAHWEH), Son (Jesus Christ) and Holy Spirit, therefore, He was consulting with Himself. And God would create man in His image, meaning our makeup is similar to God's makeup.

The Makeup of Man		
Body	Soul	**Spirit**

The Makeup of Mankind		
Spirit	Soul	**Body**

Notice in the makeup of man, the body is the most pronounced part of the man. This represents his flesh. Genesis 2:4-7 states, "These are the generations of the heavens and of the earth when they were created, in the day that the LORD God made the earth and the heavens, and every plant of the field before it was in the earth, and every herb of the field before it grew: for the LORD God had not caused it to rain upon the earth, and <u>there was not a man</u> to till the ground. But there went up a mist from the earth, and watered the whole face of the ground. And the <u>LORD God formed man of the dust of the ground,</u> and breathed into his nostrils the breath of life; and man became a living soul." After the fall of man, you'll notice that some translations of the Bible then began to refer to humans as "mankind." This means that we are a "kind of man" or, better yet, a deviation or a perverted version of what God initially created us to be. Of course, we have sin to thank for that. We have become a hybrid: a cross between two creations, and as believers, only one side of our being will spend eternity with God. Our flesh, on the other hand, has no inheritance with God (see 1 Corinthians 15:50). As a reminder, humans are eternal creatures, so when we pass away and leave the limitations of time, our spirits need a forever home. Those of us who have accepted Jesus Christ as our Lord and Savior will spend eternity in the presence of God. Unbelievers will spend eternity in the fire that burns with brimstone. This isn't to sound self-righteous; this is scriptural! But there has been a lot of debate concerning the phrases "Heaven" and "Kingdom of God." While most theologians argue that the two are synonymous, there is evidence in the scriptures that they are not. First and foremost, Heaven and Earth, according to the scriptures, will pass away, and a new Heaven and a new Earth will arise.

- **Isaiah 65:17:** For, behold, I create new heavens and a new earth: and the former shall not be remembered, nor come into mind.
- **Matthew 24:25:** Heaven and earth shall pass away, but my words shall not pass away.
- **2 Peter 3:13:** But according to his promise we are waiting for new heavens and a new earth in which righteousness dwells.
- **Revelation 21:1:** And I saw a new heaven and a new earth: for the first heaven and the first earth were passed away; and there was no more sea.

In the beginning, God created the Heaven and the Earth. Isaiah 66:1 reads, "Thus saith the LORD, The heaven is my throne, and the earth is my footstool: where is the house that ye build unto me? And where is the place of my rest?" Where is a throne typically placed? In a castle, right? Could this mean that while Heaven is in the Kingdom of God, which is why they are often used interchangeably, Heaven is not the full representation of God's Kingdom? God is eternal and He would need an eternal abode, but Heaven and Earth will pass away, and a new Heaven and Earth will replace them. All the same, the phrase "Kingdom of God" is mentioned 68 times in the New Testament, whereas, the phrase "Kingdom of Heaven" is exclusively mentioned in the book of Matthew, and it's mentioned 32 times. This isn't to challenge your theology, my goal here is to make you think and study the Word all the more. What you'll come to discover is the Kingdom of God represents God's domain. It's the full will of God on display; it's His system, His mind and all that He represents housed in a particular setting. Our hearts are divided into domains, and whenever we invite God (not just His name, but His full will) into certain areas of our hearts, we are simultaneously volunteering to host the Kingdom of God in that area of our lives. And it is in those areas that we will thrive. Heaven, on the other hand, has three realms. They are: the first Heaven, the second Heaven and the third Heaven. Please look at the chart below to get a better understanding.

First Heaven	Second Heaven	Third Heaven
Earth's Atmosphere	Outer Space	Throne of God

How do we know there are three Heavens? Let's look at a few scriptures.

- **2 Corinthians 12:2:** I knew a man in Christ above fourteen years ago, (whether in the body, I cannot tell; or whether out of the body, I cannot tell: God knoweth;) such an one caught up to the third heaven.
- **Psalm 2:4:** He that sitteth in the heavens shall laugh: the Lord shall have them in derision.
- **Deuteronomy 10:14:** Behold, the heaven and the

heaven of heavens is the LORD'S thy God, the
earth also, with all that therein is.

- **1 Kings 8:27:** But will God indeed dwell on the earth?
  Behold, the heaven and heaven of heavens cannot
  contain thee; how much less this house that I have
  builded?
- **2 Chronicles 2:6:** But who is able to build him an
  house, seeing the heaven and heaven of heavens
  cannot contain him?

As we can see, the scriptures repeatedly mention the
"heaven of heavens," meaning there is more than one
Heaven. Howbeit, it is the will of God and the Word of God
that lasts forever, even when Heaven and Earth pass away.
This would mean that the throne of God (third Heaven) is not
the resting place of God, it is His domain or His place of rule.
Consider what Lucifer said in his heart before being evicted
from Heaven. Isaiah 14:13-15 reads, "For thou hast said in
thine heart, I will ascend into heaven, I will exalt my throne
above the stars of God: I will sit also upon the mount of the
congregation, in the sides of the north: I will ascend above
the heights of the clouds; I will be like the most High. Yet
thou shalt be brought down to hell, to the sides of the pit."
Wait! Why would Lucifer plot to ascend into Heaven and
above the heights of the clouds if he was already in Heaven?
Isn't this where the infamous war took place?! The answer is
right in our faces! The second Heaven is where angels ruled!
This is why they are referred to as "stars" in Revelation 12:4,
which reads, "And his tail drew the third part of the stars of

heaven, and did cast them to the earth: and the dragon stood before the woman which was ready to be delivered, for to devour her child as soon as it was born." Of course, this scripture is detailing the fall of Satan and his angels, what we've come to now refer to as demons. Lucifer's plan was to elevate or promote himself into the third Heaven, where he planned to rule alongside God, and in some instances, in place of God. In the second Heaven, however, Lucifer started a revolution. He lied and manipulated one-third of God's angels. And what was their punishment? They were kicked out of the second Heaven!

- **Luke 10:18:** And he said unto them, I beheld Satan as lightning fall from heaven.
- **Revelation 12:7-10:** And there was war in heaven: Michael and his angels fought against the dragon; and the dragon fought and his angels, and prevailed not; neither was their place found any more in heaven. And the great dragon was cast out, that old serpent, called the Devil, and Satan, which deceiveth the whole world: he was cast out into the earth, and his angels were cast out with him. And I heard a loud voice saying in heaven, Now is come salvation, and strength, and the kingdom of our God, and the power of his Christ: for the accuser of our brethren is cast down, which accused them before our God day and night.

When did the Kingdom of God enter Heaven? When the Devil (Satan) who'd deceived the entire world was cast into the Earth along with his angels! This means that the Kingdom of God rests where the will of God exists. And we all know that God reigns forever, which means that His Kingdom is eternal. Additionally, hell and the kingdom of darkness aren't synonymous. The hosts of the kingdom of darkness will be tossed into hell, and hell will be tossed into the lake that burns with fire and brimstone. And as for darkness, it is simply overcome by light. It is void of matter, therefore, darkness isn't necessarily evil; it's just the place that Satan (temporarily) dwells because he cannot be in the presence (glory, illumination, light or will) of the Most High God.

The Establishment of Time

Genesis 1:1 reads, "In the beginning God created the heaven and the earth." When did God create the Heaven and the Earth? In the beginning, right? But what if I told you that the question that should have been posed is, where did God create Heaven and Earth, and not when? This is because the establishment of time did not take place when God created the space that we now live. When the author says, "in the beginning," He isn't referencing time, the author is referencing a location. In Revelation 21:26, we get an understanding of the term "beginning." The scripture reads, "And he said unto me, It is done. I am Alpha and Omega, the beginning and the end. I will give unto him that is athirst of the fountain of the water of life freely." Of course, this is YAHWEH Himself speaking, and who does He reference Himself as?

1. Alpha (the Beginning)
2. Omega (the End)

What does this mean? It's simple. God created the Heaven and the Earth inside of Himself! This then brings about the question, when did time begin to exist? To answer this question, we must first get an understanding regarding the purpose of time. Time is designed to mark the beginning and the end of a thing. God, Himself doesn't have a beginning, nor does He have an end. He is eternal, however, He is the Beginning (the Creator) of all things, just as He is Omega (the Judge) of all things. This is to say that He Himself exists outside of time because there is no record of His birth date since He has always existed, and there will never be a record of His end since He will always exist. But what did God want to place the constraints of time on? The days, of course. He'd created the Earth, and Earth existed outside of time. As a matter of fact, time did not exist when the Earth was created. Genesis 1:3-5 marks the moment when God placed Chronos time in the Earth. It reads, "And God said, Let there be light: and there was light. And God saw the light, that it was good: and God divided the light from the darkness. And God called the light Day, and the darkness he called Night. And the evening and the morning were the first day." Notice here that God called the light Day and the darkness Night. What He was doing here was giving darkness permission to exist. How so? Genesis 1:2 reads, "And the earth was without form, and void; and darkness was upon the face of the deep. And the Spirit of God moved upon the face of the waters." Darkness was already upon the face of the Earth. But what is darkness? Is it evil? Does this mean that evil spirits were already in the Earth? Theologians have wrestled with theories surrounding the concept of darkness for years, but the answer has been right under our noses all along. This mystery is solved in 1 John 1:5, which reads, "This then is the message which we have heard of him, and declare unto you, that God is light, and in him is no darkness at all." Now remember, in the beginning, God created the Heaven and the Earth. After this, God said, "Let there be light." Notice that He didn't say, "Let there be darkness." Instead, He separated the light from the darkness. He separated what He'd created from something that was antithetical to His being. But hear me—contrary to popular belief, darkness was not and is not in and of itself "evil." It simply means that it is a space that is untouched by God. Who is God? The Bible refers to Him as Light. This doesn't mean that the light outside is God; this is more of a characteristic or trait of God. Wherever He is, there is illumination. Wherever He is, there are no mysteries or secrets, but where He is not, there is darkness. Darkness is not matter. Scientists often refer to it as "dark matter," but it does not possess matter. Darkness has no existence to speak of. It simply means void. So, when light comes, darkness does not flee. Instead, it is simply overcome. Another way to say this is, it yields itself or bows down to light. It is overshadowed by the presence of light.

When God created the Earth, He created light to rule the day, but He also allowed darkness to continue to rule, and the space He gave darkness to rule, He called night. And it would be the space of the night where man would be required (not mandated) to rest from the work he'd done during the day. This is also the establishment of a spectrum. On any given spectrum, there are two choices that are antithetical to one another. They are the extremes often found to the left and right of a spectrum. And when there is a spectrum, there has to be the presence of "will." This means that anything and anyone who finds itself, himself or herself on a spectrum has the ability to make a choice. This would mean that before God created man, He created space for him, and within that space existed the need for will-power. But with the ability to choose, there also had to be another system or law that would regulate our choices. This system is called sowing and reaping. But how could God, Himself help us to understand the concept of sowing and reaping? It's simple. He needed to create a garden. He decided to create the Garden of Eden. This means that man had to be placed in time since both day and night now existed, and man now had the technology of will-power. But what good is will if man cannot make a choice? So, after creating Adam, God had to position him and then give him a command. Genesis 2:15-17 reads, "And the LORD God took the man, and put him into the garden of Eden to dress it and to keep it. And the LORD God commanded the man, saying, Of every tree of the garden thou mayest freely eat: But of the tree of the knowledge of good and evil, thou shalt not eat of it: for in the day that thou eatest thereof thou shalt surely die." We have to pay attention to the scriptures. God said to Adam, "But of the tree of the knowledge of good and evil, thou SHOULD NOT eat." This is what "shalt" means; it means should. Did God say that Adam could not eat from the tree? No. Adam had the technology of will-power. God said (in modern terms), "I give you permission to eat from any of the trees in this garden that I've created, but regarding the Tree of the Knowledge of Good and Evil, I don't want you to touch it or any of its fruit because the day you eat from that tree, you will die." God pretty much was saying here that the Tree of the Knowledge of Good and Evil was a tree that did not belong to His garden or system. It was not within the jurisdiction of His will. Imagine it this way. Envision a garden illuminated by day. It is a beautiful and orderly garden, but envision a line, and on the other side of that line is pitch darkness. In the darkness, you can see a tree blowing in the winds. God points to that tree and says, "You shouldn't touch that. I am good, but that's not good. To touch it, you have to step outside of my will, and to eat from it, you have to enter into an agreement with my enemy." Please understand that if God had given Adam a strict command to not touch that particular tree, Adam would have been completely in rebellion, and more than likely, he would not have been given the opportunity to redeem himself. Instead, Adam stepped outside of God's will, along with his wife, and entered into a different agreement. Jesus would come along and give mankind the ability to step back into the will of God, but in order for this event to take place, we needed Chronos time.

The purpose of time is order. God is an orderly God. What times does is it allows us to make a choice, and then it allows us to reap the benefits or consequences of that choice. In short, it allows us to decide who we want to serve, especially since there are two antithetical systems present. Let's revisit the concept of a spectrum. On one end of the spectrum, there is good; on the other end of that same spectrum is evil. On one end of a spectrum, there is light, but on the other end of that spectrum is darkness. The space in the middle of each spectrum is called a process. This process is what we call time. To the extreme left and the extreme right of each choice is an event called eternity. There is a pleasant side of eternity and a not-so-pleasant side of eternity. God teaches us, through His Word, how to get to the good side of eternity.

Again, the purpose of time is order, but not necessarily the way we think of order. Order is the arrangement of events, all of which take place as a direct result of a choice. For example, God told Adam to dress and keep the land. This is because God had already placed within the land all the seeds needed to produce a harvest. The land represented the earth or the ground, which is what Adam was made of. So, Adam's assignment was to till his flesh or to keep his flesh in submission. But to do this, he would have to water the good seeds that were already in him and avoid allowing evil to plant seeds in him. Evil had no access to him, but he had access to evil in the form of a tree. Again, he would have to step outside of order; that is, outside of God's will to even touch that tree. And when he did, he stepped into consequence, and the same system that had been present in God's will was also present outside of God's will, and that is the system or the law of sowing and reaping. Nevertheless, outside of God's will, that system would produce the fruit of death; that is, eternal separation from God, after all, it is not possible for us to have the best of both worlds. We cannot be citizens of two systems; in the spiritual world, dual citizenship simply does not exist! The minute Adam and Eve stepped outside of God's will, they stepped into darkness; this is the space ruled by Satan. As a reminder, darkness in and of itself is not evil; it simply means that it is a space not occupied by God. Satan and his angels, on the other hand, are evil, and they have to exist outside of God's presence or will. God is life, so outside of His will exists death. On the spectrum that exists outside of God's will, you will find death. To be alive means to exist in the will of God, to die simply means to cease to exist in the will of God. This means that death is an eternal separation from God; this is why Jesus had to step into time to redeem us. When Adam and Eve sinned, they died. They could no longer live in God's presence, but in the space of time, God promised to send mankind a Redeemer. The Redeemer would present us with another contract or another opportunity to choose God over His enemy. But to do this, mankind would have to follow order; we would first find ourselves in the crutches and clinches of the Old Mosaic Law, which would, at minimum, keep us familiar with and intentional towards God. But the law only served to condemn mankind. In other words, we needed a Savior, and He would have to step into time and submit and surrender Himself to time in order to redeem us. This would mean that He, too, would have to die. Because on this side of time, there is an end, an escape, or a black hole that leads to eternity, and it's called death. Howbeit, death outside of Jesus would be an eternal separation from God. This is why mankind, through the law, had to repeatedly deny himself in order to stay in connection with God. We still have to do this today, however, we have eternal life in Christ Jesus if we confess Him as our

Lord and Savior AND we serve Him. This puts us on the other side of the time spectrum, whereas we have been reconciled with God through His Son.

Let's discuss the establishment of Chronos time as we know it. I'm talking about calendars, watches and schedules. The following article was taken from Scientific American®.

"According to archaeological evidence, the Babylonians and Egyptians began to measure time at least 5,000 years ago, introducing calendars to organize and coordinate communal activities and public events, to schedule the shipment of goods and, in particular, to regulate cycles of planting and harvesting. They based their calendars on three natural cycles: the solar day, marked by the successive periods of light and darkness as the earth rotates on its axis; the lunar month, following the phases of the moon as it orbits the earth; and the solar year, defined by the changing seasons that accompany our planet's revolution around the sun. Before the invention of artificial light, the moon had greater social impact. And, for those living near the equator in particular, its waxing and waning was more conspicuous than the passing of the seasons. Hence, the calendars developed at the lower latitudes were influenced more by the lunar cycle than by the solar year. In more northern climes, however, where seasonal agriculture was important, the solar year became more crucial. As the Roman Empire expanded northward, it organized its calendar for the most part around the solar year. Today's Gregorian calendar derives from the Babylonian, Egyptian, Jewish and Roman calendars.

The Egyptians formulated a civil calendar having 12 months of 30 days, with five days added to approximate the solar year. Each period of 10 days was marked by the appearance of special star groups (constellations) called decans. At the rise of the star Sirius just before sunrise, which occurred around the all-important annual flooding of the Nile, 12 decans could be seen spanning the heavens. The cosmic significance the Egyptians placed in the 12 decans led them to develop a system in which each interval of darkness (and later, each interval of daylight) was divided into a dozen equal parts. These periods became known as temporal hours because their duration varied according to the changing length of days and nights with the passing of the seasons. Summer hours were long, winter ones short; only at the spring and autumn equinoxes were the hours of daylight and darkness equal. Temporal hours, which were adopted by the Greeks and then the Romans (who spread them throughout Europe), remained in use for more than 2,500 years.

Inventors created sundials, which indicate time by the length or direction of the sun's shadow, to track temporal hours during the day. The sundial's nocturnal counterpart, the water clock, was designed

to measure temporal hours at night. One of the first water clocks was a basin with a small hole near the bottom through which the water dripped out. The falling water level denoted the passing hour as it dipped below hour lines inscribed on the inner surface. Although these devices performed satisfactorily around the Mediterranean, they could not always be depended on in the cloudy and often freezing weather of northern Europe."
(Source: American Scientific®/A Chronicle of Timekeeping/William H. Andrewes)

First and foremost, this shows that the Babylonians did not create time, they simply acknowledged and recorded its existence. Their reasoning for this was so that they could better predict the weather patterns, organize events and so they could master the art of farming. Of course, over time, they started introducing things like astrology and astronomy in their attempts to better understand time and its effects on the Earth. Like most of us, the Babylonians noticed weather patterns. They noticed that the weather would repeat certain patterns at certain times. They noticed the behavior of the plants, the sun, the moon and the animals. To survive longer and to thrive, they needed to master time. This is why they created the calendars that we use today.

Mark Your Calendar

On your cellphone, you will likely find a calendar app. If you press the icon to open the app, all you will find is a Gregorian calendar listing all the days of this month. You can click on certain points of the calendar to see the year that you're in, to look at other months or years, either past or futuristic, and you can mark your calendar. This would allow you to place a reminder in your phone and to get your phone to notify you when that particular event is approaching. The event can be something as minute as a phone call, a doctor's appointment, or something as grand as a wedding. Either way, populating our calendars is our way of saying that we believe that we will be alive on that particular day and we'll be healthy enough to participate in that particular event. But what is a calendar, and why do we need it? Before we answer this question, let's reflect on the concept of time itself.

As a reminder, God created the light, and He called this space of time Day. He then separated it from the darkness; this is the space of time He called Night. To allow them both the ability to rule, God had to place time constraints on each one. During the Summer months, daytime lasts more than 12 hours, but during the Winter months, daytime lasts less than 12 hours. This means that the darkness rules most of the time during the Winter months (in certain hemispheres), while the day rules most of the time in the Summer months (in certain hemispheres). And we have to know what spaces of time we're in if we want to survive and flourish. For example, you wouldn't want to wear a tank-top in the dead of Winter. If you did this, you could easily fall victim to hypothermia. All the same, you wouldn't want to wear a coat in the middle of Summer, especially in the South. If you did this, you would fall prey to a heat stroke. This means that understanding the times is important. And again, knowing your own individual self and the patterns of your life will help you to better manage yourself, your life and your results. This is why people who don't have a handle on their emotions tend to experience more depression and more calamities than the people who've come to better understand themselves, their habits, their patterns and how they interact with certain times, things and people. A great example of this would be the classic introvert. An individual who does not know that he or she is an introvert is a person who will likely misjudge or misdiagnose himself or herself. For example, let's say that Tim is an introvert, but he doesn't know this. We live in a world where extroversion is considered normal, but introversion is considered relatively abnormal. This means that most of the people around Tim are extroverts. Tim would see these people on social media posting pictures of their very active social lives. But whenever he attempted to mingle with a few friends of his, he would find himself mentally and physically drained. All the same, because most of his friends would be extroverts, they would question him and cause him to question himself about his need to break away from people after two or more hours. Consequently,

Tim would think that there was something wrong with him. He'd probably throw away thousands of dollars undergoing counseling sessions that he does not need. Additionally, he'd likely force himself to go out more, which would ultimately render him incapable of enjoying the life that God set aside for him because he'd spend most of his alone time feeling drained. But knowing and understanding his own makeup would allow Tim to flourish in an extrovert's world. This is because Tim, like you and me, is a gift, but every gift is not for everyone, nor is it for every season. Consider the life of Daniel. A prophet of the Most High God, Daniel had once lived in Jerusalem. There, he was gifted, but he wasn't necessarily a gift because his gift of prophecy was not being utilized. In today's language, Daniel had been kidnapped and held against his will in a foreign land. And it was in Babylon that Daniel's gift began to activate. This is because a gift's light shines brightest in the darkness!

Daniel 1:1-7 tells the story of Daniel's rise to fame. It reads, "In the third year of the reign of Jehoiakim king of Judah came Nebuchadnezzar king of Babylon unto Jerusalem, and besieged it. And the Lord gave Jehoiakim king of Judah into his hand, with part of the vessels of the house of God: which he carried into the land of Shinar to the house of his god; and he brought the vessels into the treasure house of his god. And the king spake unto Ashpenaz the master of his eunuchs, that he should bring certain of the children of Israel, and of the king's seed, and of the princes; children in whom was no blemish, but well favoured, and skilful in all

47

wisdom, and cunning in knowledge, and understanding science, and such as had ability in them to stand in the king's palace, and whom they might teach the learning and the tongue of the Chaldeans. And the king appointed them a daily provision of the king's meat, and of the wine which he drank: so nourishing them three years, that at the end thereof they might stand before the king. Now among these were of the children of Judah, Daniel, Hananiah, Mishael, and Azariah: Unto whom the prince of the eunuchs gave names: for he gave unto Daniel the name of Belteshazzar; and to Hananiah, of Shadrach; and to Mishael, of Meshach; and to Azariah, of Abednego."

As you may very well know, Daniel ends up interpreting King Nebuchadnezzar's dream, and because of this, he was promoted. King Nebuchadnezzar set Daniel over the entire province of Babylon, and Daniel would go on to appoint Shadrach, Meshach, and Abednego as his aids. Howbeit, many of the Babylonian men found themselves feeling jealous of Daniel and his aids. Let's look at that particular story.

Daniel 3:3-6: Then the princes, the governors, and captains, the judges, the treasurers, the counsellers, the sheriffs, and all the rulers of the provinces, were gathered together unto the dedication of the image that Nebuchadnezzar the king had set up; and they stood before the image that Nebuchadnezzar had set up. Then an herald cried aloud, To you it is commanded, O people, nations, and

48

languages, That at what time ye hear the sound of the cornet, flute, harp, sackbut, psaltery, dulcimer, and all kinds of musick, ye fall down and worship the golden image that Nebuchadnezzar the king hath set up: And whoso falleth not down and worshippeth shall the same hour be cast into the midst of a burning fiery furnace.

Daniel 3:8-12: Wherefore at that time certain Chaldeans came near, and accused the Jews. They spake and said to the king Nebuchadnezzar, O king, live for ever. Thou, O king, hast made a decree, that every man that shall hear the sound of the cornet, flute, harp, sackbut, psaltery, and dulcimer, and all kinds of musick, shall fall down and worship the golden image: And whoso falleth not down and worshippeth, that he should be cast into the midst of a burning fiery furnace. There are certain Jews whom thou hast set over the affairs of the province of Babylon, Shadrach, Meshach, and Abednego; these men, O king, have not regarded thee: they serve not thy gods, nor worship the golden image which thou hast set up.

The three men would be tossed into a fiery furnace, but they would survive. King Nebuchadnezzar would repent of tossing them into the fire, but Daniel's problems would be far from over. You see, Daniel was a gift, and a gift's gifting works best in difficult times. Think of it this way. Why would you need a flashlight in the daytime? If darkness didn't exist, we wouldn't need light bulbs. What we find happening in the book of Daniel is that a new king comes on the scene, and

Daniel also had favor with this king. As always, this upset some of the people surrounding the king, and they decided that they wanted to change the king's views about Daniel in hopes that Daniel would be killed.

Daniel 6:1-8: It pleased Darius to set over the kingdom an hundred and twenty princes, which should be over the whole kingdom; and over these three presidents; of whom Daniel was first: that the princes might give accounts unto them, and the king should have no damage. Then this Daniel was preferred above the presidents and princes, because an excellent spirit was in him; and the king thought to set him over the whole realm. Then the presidents and princes sought to find occasion against Daniel concerning the kingdom; but they could find none occasion nor fault; forasmuch as he was faithful, neither was there any error or fault found in him. Then said these men, We shall not find any occasion against this Daniel, except we find it against him concerning the law of his God. Then these presidents and princes assembled together to the king, and said thus unto him, King Darius, live for ever. All the presidents of the kingdom, the governors, and the princes, the counsellers, and the captains, have consulted together to establish a royal statute, and to make a firm decree, that whosoever shall ask a petition of any God or man for thirty days, save of thee, O king, he shall be cast into the den of lions. Now, O king, establish the decree, and sign the writing, that it be not changed, according to the law of the Medes and Persians, which altereth not. Wherefore king Darius signed the writing and the decree.

Of course, the decree was established and Daniel was eventually tossed into the lion's den, where he would survive. As for the men who'd allowed their jealousy to get the best of them, Daniel 6:24 details their fate. "And the king commanded, and they brought those men which had accused Daniel, and they cast them into the den of lions, them, their children, and their wives; and the lions had the mastery of them, and brake all their bones in pieces or ever they came at the bottom of the den." And again, this does not end Daniel's story, but it helps us to better understand the times of a gift. Daniel was a gift who was gifted. His gift was not needed in Jerusalem; his gift was needed in Babylon. Howbeit, while there, like many other gifts, Daniel would find that he would be repeatedly challenged by men who, simply put, felt entitled to his gifting, his position and his favor. This all happened during Daniel's lifetime, believed to be 620–538 B.C. Daniel had been born when his particular set of skills and giftings would be needed. The same is true for you. You are alive to read this today, but this does not mean that your gift is needed right now. Then again, where you are geographically located may be hindering your gift! If God tells you to move, you have to do like Abram and move, or like Daniel and Joseph, you could be potentially forced out of your comfort zone so that God could activate your gift. There is a specific day and hour in which your gift should be on full display, but this cannot and will not happen if you aren't positioned in the right places geographically, mentally and spiritually. Galatians 4:1-5 confirms this; it reads, "Now I say, That the heir, as long as he is a child, differeth nothing from a servant, though he be lord of all; but is under tutors and governors until the time appointed of the father. Even so we, when we were children, were in bondage under the elements of the world: But when the fulness of the time was come, God sent forth his Son, made of a woman, made under the law, to redeem them that were under the law, that we might receive the adoption of sons."

The Greek word for "child" is "népios," and it literally means "unlearned." This is just another way of saying immature. As believers, we are all heirs of Christ, but according to Galatians 4, as long as we are unlearned, immature or babes in Christ, we cannot tap into or access certain parts of our inheritance. According to the scriptures, as long as we are "children," we are in bondage to the elements of this world. This means that we are carnal in our thinking, immature, sensual and foolish. And yet, we are lord of all, meaning we have all of Heaven and Earth at our fingertips, but we cannot access them the way we want to because of our immaturity. So, while there are calendared events scheduled to take place in our lives, we can and do cause the delays that we complain about when we don't study so that we can show ourselves approved for the miracles, signs, wonders and blessings that we covet. This also means that while we are "children," we are law-minded. In other words, we have a tendency to be transactional towards God, works-driven and fearful. This is why the scriptures also tell us that perfect love casts out fear (see 1 John 4:18). The word "perfect" in this scripture doesn't mean without flaw, it means mature love. I say all this to say that, as believers, we have to stop being calendar-minded, meaning we have to stop being entitled, thinking that certain events will automatically take place just because we are Christians or just because we have religious titles.

We've seen it many times. A flyer populates on social media, and on the face of that flyer, we see a group of faces, some may be familiar, others are unfamiliar to us. And nestled just towards the bottom of the flyer, we see those famous words, "Mark your calendars!" The big, bold exclamation point is designed to heighten our interest in the event; the hosts of the event want to draw excitement and expectation around the event so that people will register. Howbeit, we look at the faces on the flyer to determine if we truly believe that the conference or whatever it is that they are hosting is worth the time, money and effort required to attend. If we don't think it's worth it, we won't bother with registering. If we do think it's worth it, we first have to look at our own personal calendars or schedules to see if we can go. All the same, in order for this particular event to take place, the hosts need:

1. To book a venue.
2. To reserve the speakers for the venue.
3. To purchase, rent or possess the technology that will be needed for the venue, including microphones, cameras, television prompts, etc.
4. To reserve skilled people who can work all of the

equipment used at the event.
5. To have an audience.

All of this takes time and money. If all of these things are not in place, the hosts will likely have to cancel the event, and this is not unheard of. It happens all the time. This is because the calendar allows the host to set a date aside to have the event, but as with all things, everything needs to be in order if the event is to be a successful one. Howbeit, before we can talk about the needs of a gift, let's get an understanding of what we've come to know as a calendar.

What exactly is a calendar, and what is its purpose? According to Merriam Webster, a "calendar" is "a system for fixing the beginning, length, and divisions of the civil year and arranging days and longer divisions of time (such as weeks and months) in a definite order." The following information was taken from The Old Farmer's Almanac:

"Today, we follow the Gregorian calendar, but it's based on the ancient Roman calendar, believed to be invented by Romulus, who served as the first king of Rome around 753 BC.

The Roman calendar, a complicated lunar calendar, had 12 months like our current calendar, but only 10 of the months had formal names. Basically, winter was a "dead" period of time when the government and military wasn't active, so they only had names for the time period we think of as March through December. March (Martius) was named for Mars, the god of war, because this was the month when active military campaigns resumed. May (Maius) and June (Junius) were also named for goddesses: Maia and Juno. April (Aprilis) is thought to stem from Latin aperio, meaning "to open"—a reference to the opening buds of springtime. The rest of the months were simply numbered; their original names in Latin meant the fifth (Quintilis), sixth (Sextilis), seventh (September), eighth (October), ninth (November), and tenth (December) month.

Eventually, January (Januarius) and February (Februarius) were added to the end of the year, giving all 12 months proper names. January was named after Janus, the Roman god of beginnings and transitions, while February's name is believed to stem from Februa, an ancient festival dedicated to ritual springtime cleaning and washing.

Julian Calendar Updates

When Julius Caesar became pontifex maximus, he reformed the Roman calendar so that the 12 months were based on Earth's revolutions around the Sun. It was a solar calendar as we have today. January and February were moved to the front of the year, and leap years were introduced to keep the calendar year lined up with the solar year.

The winter months (January and February) remained a time of reflection, peace, new beginnings, and purification. After Caesar's death, the month

Quintilis was renamed July in honor of Julius Caesar in 44 BC and, later, Sextilis was renamed August in honor of Roman Emperor Augustus in 8 BC.

Of course, all the renaming and reorganizing meant that some of the months' names no longer agreed with their position in the calendar (September to December, for example). Later emperors tried to name various months after themselves, but those changes did not outlive them!

Today's Gregorian Calendar

Quite a bit later, in 1582, Pope Gregory XIII introduced a number of reforms to the Julian calendar, as there were still some inaccuracies and adjustments to be made. Mainly, the Julian calendar had overestimated the amount of time it took the Earth to orbit the Sun, so the Gregorian calendar shortened the calendar year from 365.25 days to 365.2425 days. This meant that the calendar could be more easily corrected by leap years and that the dates of the equinoxes and solstices—and thus, the date of Easter— once again lined up with their observed dates."

(Source: The Old Farmer's Almanac/How Did the Months Get Their Names?/Catherine Boeckmann)

The goal of the calendar, frankly put, is to organize time. It allowed mankind to become better at predicting events, establish and observe religious or sacred moments and events, and it allowed us to create schedules, set appointments and measure one another's competency. It also allowed us to set reasonable expectations, for example, in Western society, we have determined that the legal age of adulthood is 18-years old, and the legal age for drinking is 21-years old. These laws are different in other countries. This means that a human will have to have existed for a total of 216 months before that individual is considered by the law as an adult. Without the ordering or organization of time, we would be left to make this determination on our own or by using other devices. By establishing a standard age or time, our justice system could rule more fairly, and every other system that we establish could be better protected and preserved by our one-sized-fits-all rules, standards, laws and requirements.

There are three main types of calendars being used around the world today. They are:

1. **Solar:** A solar calendar is a calendar whose dates indicate the season or almost equivalently the apparent position of the Sun relative to the stars. The Gregorian calendar, widely accepted as a standard in the world, is an example of a solar calendar. The main other type of calendar is a lunar calendar, whose months correspond to cycles of Moon phases. The months of the Gregorian calendar do not correspond to cycles of the Moon phase (Source: Wikipedia).

2. **Lunar:** A lunar calendar is a calendar based on the monthly cycles of the Moon's phases (synodic

months, lunations), in contrast to solar calendars, whose annual cycles are based only directly on the solar year. The most commonly used calendar, the Gregorian calendar, is a solar calendar system that originally evolved out of a lunar calendar system. A purely lunar calendar is also distinguished from a lunisolar calendar, whose lunar months are brought into alignment with the solar year through some process of intercalation. The details of when months begin varies from calendar to calendar, with some using new, full, or crescent moons and others employing detailed calculations (Source: Wikipedia).

3. **Lunisolar/Solilunar:** A lunisolar calendar is a calendar in many cultures whose date indicates both the Moon phase and the time of the solar year. If the solar year is defined as a tropical year, then a lunisolar calendar will give an indication of the season; if it is taken as a sidereal year, then the calendar will predict the constellation near which the full moon may occur. As with all calendars which divide the year into months, there is an additional requirement that the year have a whole number of months. In this case, ordinary years consist of twelve months, but every second or third year is an embolismic year, which adds a thirteenth intercalary, embolismic, or leap month. Their months are based on the regular cycle of the Moon's phases. So lunisolar calendars are lunar calendars with – in contrast to them – additional intercalation rules being

used to bring them into a rough agreement with the solar year and thus with the seasons (Source: Wikipedia).

We currently use a solar calendar called the Gregorian Calendar. The Gregorian Calendar was established by Gregory XIII, also known as Ugo Boncompagni. Gregory XIII was a Catholic pope from 1572 to 1585. He established the Gregorian Calendar in 1585 as a replacement for the Julian Calendar. He believed that the time on the Julian calendar was slightly off. The Julian calendar was comprised of 365.25 days, but a solar year was comprised of 365 days, 5 hours, 48 minutes, 45.25 seconds. This caused us to lose almost one day every century.

The point that I want to make is that time is important, and while time was created by God to establish order and to help us better understand the law of sowing and reaping, time has to be ordered or, better yet, organized. In other words, we have to understand time to make the best use of it. The same is true for us individually. Every human is submitted to time, but we are all different. As an individual, it is important for you to recognize the patterns that show up in your own life. This is what we call self-management. This is what a farmer has to do. He has to monitor his gardens to see the behavior of each of the fruits, vegetables and legumes that he plants. This allows him to know when to water and fertilize the ground, and it tells him how much water and fertilizer he needs to put down. All the same, understanding each individual fruit allows the gardener to use the right kind and amount of pesticide. This is why you cannot measure your life by the results of someone else. What one individual needs to sustain his or her own life may be too much for you or too little. This is why jealousy and covetousness are both asinine. Remember, this is why the men who accused the prophet Daniel ended up in the lions' den themselves. They were oranges wishing they could be apples. If you were an orange tree monitoring and comparing yourself to an apple tree, you would be doing yourself a great disservice. For example, an apple tree must be watered every 7-10 days, but an orange tree has to be watered twice a week. This would mean that the marks you place on your personal calendar cannot match the marks I place on my own or what someone else places on their own. You are a unique gift, and as such, God has a diet that is custom created just for you. Your particular diet will allow you to flourish at your maximum capacity in your set time. Howbeit, when you submit yourself to the preferences and needs of another gift, you will either cause yourself to over-perform and burnout or to under-perform and fall behind.

"The jealous are troublesome to others, but a torment to themselves."

~William Penn

The Kingdom Makeup of a Gift

The Hebrew word for "create" is "bara." Strong's Concordance (#1254) defines it this way:

> a primitive root; (absolutely) to create; (qualified) to cut down (a wood), select, feed (as formative processes):-- choose, create (creator), cut down, dispatch, do, make (fat).

In Genesis 1, we find God creating. This is why we reference Him as the Creator of all things. He created the Earth and everything in it, and He did this by creating a series of systems and processes that are all interconnected. For example, He created the human body, but not before creating the spirit of the human. Genesis 1:26-27 records the moment when the human spirit was created. It reads, "And God said, Let us make man in our image, after our likeness: and let them have dominion over the fish of the sea, and over the fowl of the air, and over the cattle, and over all the earth, and over every creeping thing that creepeth upon the earth. So God created man in his own image, in the image of God created he him; male and female created he them." But notice that God had not formed the body of the human. He didn't do this until Genesis 2:6-7, which reads, "But there went up a mist from the earth, and watered the whole face of the ground. And the LORD God formed man of the dust of the ground, and breathed into his nostrils the breath of life; and man became a living soul." So here, we witness the body of Adam being created; this would serve as the container for his spirit. And once Adam's body and his spirit overlapped, his soul was created. The soul communicates or bridges the spirit with the body that it's in.

In the world of physiology, we come to understand the makeup of the human body and the many sub-systems that work together to help each individual function and survive in the Earth. These systems include, but are not limited to:

- The cardiovascular system
- The digestive system
- The endocrine system
- The lymphatic system
- The muscular system
- The nervous system
- The reproductive system
- The respiratory system
- The skeletal system
- The urinary system

These are considered the major or most important systems of the body, and while they all function independently of one another, they are all interdependent on one another, which is why they are all sub-systems that make up a system called anatomy. This is similar to our makeup in the spiritual world, but before we dive into the lesson, we must understand that we are spirits living in bodies, and we all have souls. I am not my body; you are not your body. We are spirits living in bodies. Our bodies give us the ability and the legal right to live on Earth. But we are spirits, and this is why we are spiritual. This is also why the weapons of our warfare are not carnal but mighty through God to the pulling down of strongholds (see 2 Corinthians 10:4).

Just like we have natural bodies, every gift has a spiritual body, and this body is made up of our character, our anointing and our spirit. Let's first talk about our spirits. The Greek word for "spirit" is "pneuma" and it literally means "wind" or "breath." God is Spirit. He made us in His image. How did He do this? He breathed into Adam's body, thus, making an impartation of Himself, but before He did this, He spoke man into existence.

The human body is made of matter, just like everything else on Earth. According to Encyclopedia Britannica, matter is "material substance that constitutes the observable universe and, together with energy, forms the basis of all objective phenomena." In other words, matter creates what we can see, touch, taste, hear and feel. The spirit of a person, on the other hand, is not made up of matter. This is why it cannot be necessarily referred to as energy. Energy is observable; simply put, it is the ability to do work. The following information was taken from the American Petroleum Institute, "Energy is the capacity of a system to do work. That system may be a jet carrying hundreds of passengers across the ocean. A baby's body, growing bone cells. A kite, rising on the wind. Or a wave of light crossing a space. In moving or growing, each of these systems is doing work, and using energy. Every living organism does work, and needs energy from food or photosynthesis. Humans also create machines that do work for them, and that derive energy from fuels" (Source: American Petroleum Institute/What is Energy?) This, of course, would bring about the question, what exactly is a spirit, and what is it made of? In truth, a spirit is similar to energy, even though they aren't one and the same, so it's not exactly erroneous to refer to a spirit as energy. What, however, differentiates the two is their behavior. Energy is the capacity or ability to do work; this is just potential. In order for potential to be actualized, there has to be a force behind it. Believe it or not, the forces that empower or activate the movement of energy in a human body are words. This is why Jesus said in John 6:63, "It is the spirit who gives life. The flesh profits nothing. The words that I speak to you are spirit, and are life." The energy that enforces or carries out those words is expressed through a soul. A soul is comprised of a mind, will and emotions. The mind of a human is the engine of that person's will. It is the factory where we store our thoughts, ideas and beliefs. The mind is broken up into three realms: conscious, subconscious and unconscious. The subconscious is the mixing pot; this is where our suspicions, beliefs, imaginations and ideas are housed. This is also where they meet up to form our perspectives. Our will, on the other hand, is our mode of expression. It is the utterance or pronouncing of our beliefs and the decisions that surround those beliefs. And finally, we have our emotions. These are the pulses of our decisions. When a thought, suspicion or theory meets a belief, they produce energy. This energy is called an emotion. But this is a contained energy that seeks to express itself through our will. It's very similar to blood. Blood makes its way from the heart, and it circulates throughout the entire body through vessels; this is called the circulatory system. This means that in order for blood to travel, it has to have a means of travel. The vessels provide it with the means. The same is true for emotions. Housed within the container of the mind, our emotions first express themselves to us before they are able to express themselves through us. This takes place through a series of thoughts and imaginations. These thoughts are moved by either faith or fear; these are the spiritual vessels that connect our thoughts and decisions with our will. The will is what we use to express whatever it is that we believe. This is very similar to light. Light has to have a source. The following information was taken from Science Learning Hub:

"Something that produces light is called a light source. There are two main kinds of light sources:

Incandescent sources use heat to produce light. Nearly all solids, liquids and gases will start to glow with a dull red color once they reach a temperature of about 525 °C. At about 2300 °C, the filament in a light bulb will start to produce all of the colors of the visible spectrum, so it will look white. The Sun, stars, a flame and molten metal are all incandescent.

Luminescent sources are normally cooler and can be produced by chemical reactions, such as in a glowstick or a glow-worm. Other luminescent sources include a computer screen, fluorescent lights and LEDs" (Source: Science Learning Hub/Pokapū Akoranga Pūtaiao/Light Basics).

This is to say that every form of energy needs:
1. A source
2. A will
3. A body to express itself throughout
4. A body to express itself to

The same is true for a spirit. While we can use words like "energy" or "power" to describe just what a spirit is to us; in all truth, it is a word in a container being expressed by a soul.

Genesis 1:3 reads, "And God said, Let there be light: and there was light." What we've learned from Genesis 1:1-2 is that God pretty much started with nothing; He didn't have any raw materials, but in Genesis 1:3, we see Him beginning the creational process by saying, "Let there be light." Please note that everything God creates has a purpose, or He creates for a purpose. There are three spheres of creation that we need to look at. In short:
1. **There are certain things that God creates for His pleasure.** For example, entertainment. Entertainment has no real purpose other than to entertain or to bring pleasure.
2. **There are some things that God creates to accomplish an assignment.** Adam is the perfect

example. Genesis 2:5 helps us to understand just why Adam was created; the scripture reads, "And every plant of the field before it was in the earth, and every herb of the field before it grew: for the LORD God had not caused it to rain upon the earth, and *there was* not a man to till the ground."

3. **There are some things that are made for crisis.** Consider the anointing. Genesis 3:21 reads, "Unto Adam also and to his wife did the LORD God make coats of skins, and clothed them." This means that an animal had to be skinned in order for Adam and his wife to be covered. But in order for the animal to be skinned, God created the technology of an altar. An altar is designed for crisis.

When these three overlap, they produce two spheres:
1. A creational sphere
2. A correctional sphere

Creational Sphere: In this particular sphere, we'll find a world of gifts; these are individuals who can create anything from carpets to jet skis to rockets. And they don't just create something that's visually appealing, they have to ensure that whatever it is that they create is functional. When things that are made for an assignment overlap with the things that are created for crisis, they create a correctional sphere.

Correctional Sphere: A good example of a correctional sphere are most ministries that are found in a church setting. Their goal is to fix something. Hear me—one of the most difficult assignments is to create and fix something at the same time! The example I like to use when talking about correctional ministries is absence. I pastor thousands of creatives, many of whom attend my church. Many of them serve in the church. So, one of my dilemmas is trying to create when I'm having to correct someone about their attendance. That person is trying to fix something in his or her own life, but I'm trying to fix his or her character. You see, I understand that if I can get their character in shape, everything else will fall in line, but if their priorities don't necessarily mirror my own, we (in essence) become opponents or two opposing forces, meaning we are not walking in agreement. Amos 3:3 poses the question, "Can two walk together, except they be agreed?" Where there is no agreement, force has to be applied. God does not force us to do anything, and I have to obey that same law because forcing someone to do something they don't want to do is called witchcraft. I can, however, correct them. Correction is a force within itself. It puts pressure on the will of a person. To understand this, we need to understand physics. The following information was taken from the Physics Classroom:

> "Newton's Third Law of Motion is naturally applied to collisions between two objects. In a collision between two objects, both objects experience forces that are equal in magnitude and opposite in direction. Such forces often cause one object to speed up (gain momentum) and the other object to slow down (lose momentum). According to Newton's Third Law, the forces on the two objects are equal in magnitude.

While the forces are equal in magnitude and opposite in direction, the accelerations of the objects are not necessarily equal in magnitude. In accord with Newton's Second Law of Motion, the acceleration of an object is dependent upon both force and mass. <u>Thus, if the colliding objects have unequal mass, they will have unequal accelerations as a result of the contact force that results during the collision.</u> Consider the collision between the club head and the golf ball in the sport of golf. When the club head of a moving golf club collides with a golf ball at rest upon a tee, the force experienced by the club head is equal to the force experienced by the golf ball. Most observers of this collision have difficulty with this concept because they perceive the high speed given to the ball as the result of the collision. They are not observing unequal forces upon the ball and club head, but rather unequal accelerations. Both club head and ball experience equal forces, yet the ball experiences a greater acceleration due to its smaller mass. In a collision, there is a force on both objects that causes an acceleration of both objects. The forces are equal in magnitude and opposite in direction, yet the least massive object receives the greatest acceleration" (Source: The Physics Classroom/The Law of Action-Reaction Revisited).

Notice that I underlined the following statement, "Thus, if the colliding objects have unequal mass, they will have unequal accelerations as a result of the contact force that results during the collision." In layman's terms, their decisions do affect me, however, we are not always ranked the same. Hear me—we are all equally loved by God but aren't all equally ranked by God! Rank represents mass in the realm of the spirit. This means that their decisions will have a greater impact on them than they do on me. This doesn't mean that I'm not affected by their choices because I am, but it does mean that I had to learn to think like a scientist. If an object or person is pulling, I only pull with that person if the direction he or she is pulling in reflects God's will for them. But if they are pulling in the opposite direction, I have to let go. This allows all the energy from their decisions to collide with them. If a person is pushing, I push with them if the direction they are pushing in reflects God's will for them. But if they are pushing away from God's will, I have to allow them to push alone, and like a scientist, I have to stand afar off and record the results. This doesn't mean that I don't pray for them or attempt to correct them. It simply means that they are spirits expressing themselves, and I have to ensure that I am not a spiritual vessel that is impacted, moved, hindered or harmed by their decisions. So, I have to put whatever measure of space and time between us that is needed to ensure that a domino effect doesn't take place. This is how spirits move. They express themselves through one earthly vessel (human) to another. This is why God told us not to be friends, for example, with an angry man. That spirit of anger is like a virus. It is contagious, and it needs as many vessels as possible to express itself through. This is why angry people always seek to upset the people around them. Because what's in them overwhelms them until it finds more space to express itself.

And finally, where the creational sphere and the correctional sphere overlap, you have bara. Remember, the Hebrew word for "create" is "bara." Another word for "gift" (that's you) is a "creative." Your ability to create is called potential, but your willingness to create is called obedience. Obedience is the expression of will; it is an agreement between two forces or spirits that is expressed through a decision. Within this sphere, we see the creation of things, both great and small. In this sphere, we see the birthing of inventions, books, companies and many other forms of media. This is the sphere where energy meets mass, thus, producing matter. This is what we were created for; we were created to create.

- **Genesis 2:7:** And the LORD God formed man *of* the dust of the ground, and breathed into his nostrils the breath of life; and man became a living soul.
- **Genesis 2:15:** And the LORD God took the man, and put him into the garden of Eden to dress it and to keep it.
- **Genesis 2:19-20:** And out of the ground the LORD God formed every beast of the field, and every fowl of the air; and brought *them* unto Adam to see what he would call them: and whatsoever Adam called every living creature, that *was* the name thereof. And Adam gave names to all cattle, and to the fowl of the air, and

to every beast of the field; but for Adam there was not found an help meet for him.

- **Genesis 2:21:** And the LORD God caused a deep sleep to fall upon Adam, and he slept: and he took one of his ribs, and closed up the flesh instead thereof; and the rib, which the LORD God had taken from man, made he a woman, and brought her unto the man.

What we see in this is that man is created to recreate, and then, his highest form of expression is through procreation. Procreation isn't just the making of children; it is the reproducing of the father (progenitor) that allows the father's spirit (thoughts, plans and words) to continue on the Earth, even after the father passes away. This also means that a father isn't just a sperm donor. Any man or woman who reproduces his or her plans through another person is a father (or mother). This is what it means to have the spirit of someone else. 2 Kings 2:9-15 reads, "And it came to pass, when they were gone over, that Elijah said unto Elisha, Ask what I shall do for thee, before I be taken away from thee. And Elisha said, I pray thee, let a double portion of thy spirit be upon me. And he said, Thou hast asked a hard thing: nevertheless, if thou see me when I am taken from thee, it shall be so unto thee; but if not, it shall not be so. And it came to pass, as they still went on, and talked, that, behold, there appeared a chariot of fire, and horses of fire, and parted them both asunder; and Elijah went up by a whirlwind into heaven. And Elisha saw it, and he cried, My father, my father, the chariot of Israel, and the horsemen thereof. And he saw him no more: and he took hold of his own clothes, and rent them in two pieces. He took up also the mantle of Elijah that fell from him, and went back, and stood by the bank of Jordan; and he took the mantle of Elijah that fell from him, and smote the waters, and said, Where is the LORD God of Elijah? And when he also had smitten the waters, they parted hither and thither: and Elisha went over. And when the sons of the prophets which were to view at Jericho saw him, they said, The spirit of Elijah doth rest on Elisha." What Elisha picked up wasn't Elijah's "energy" per-se, he picked up his plans, his thoughts or, better yet, his assignment. But when Elisha died, he hadn't found a successor to impart that same spirit to, so he died with his anointing intact. This means that there was not another vessel close enough to him for him to express himself through. Hear me—as a gift, it is always easy to find people to express yourself to; this is your audience, and they are called followers, but the ultimate expression of power and the culmination of every gift's life is when we express ourselves or, better yet, reproduce ourselves through others. This is not only the makeup of a gift, it is the expression or purpose of a gift!

And finally, the spirit of a gift is three-dimensional; it is comprised of:
1. Character
2. Anointing
3. Assignment

Character: The character of a gift is made up of his or her characteristics or traits. Oxford Languages defines "character" this way: "the mental and moral qualities distinctive to an individual." But character is much more than this! It's not just the mental and moral qualities that set the stage for a person's personality, it is the container in which that person houses his or her choices. Let me say it this way. Some people are atheists, but they do good things. Does this make them good? No. They were created by the Creator Himself, therefore, there is going to be some residue of His character on them, after all, we are made in His image. What force is behind their good works? For example, a woman could find herself walking down an alley and see a man following up behind a visibly upset woman. That woman could make the decision to follow the man to see if he knows the woman and to ensure that the woman in question isn't harmed. After following them for about five minutes, she yells out to the woman who's clearly trying to get away from the guy, "Do you need help?!" The woman (we'll call her Felicia) turns around and yells at the other woman (we'll call her Betty), "Help! I don't know this man!" At this moment, the strange man realizes that he's outnumbered, so he runs away, leaving the two very frightened women alone. They begin to walk together until they get to Felicia's car. Felicia then takes her new friend home. And while driving towards Betty's home, Felicia expresses to Betty that the reason she got involved is because she had been attacked while walking home one night, and her attacker had beaten her within an inch of her life. When she saw the strange man following

Betty, she felt compelled to follow him to not only ensure Betty's safety, but she wanted the man to be arrested. After this incident, Felicia makes it her personal mission to find and prosecute the man that followed Betty that night. Did she do this because she loved Betty? No. And while we don't necessarily care why she potentially could have saved another woman's life because what's important is that a life was spared, we can't confuse her decision to get involved with her being a good person. This may have been a knee-jerk reaction, meaning she did this instinctively because of what happened to her. Betty could easily become friends with Felicia and discover that she's an abusive, mentally unstable and rage-filled drug addict. So, we shouldn't confuse good deeds with character.

The character of a person is his or her moral compass and everything that comes together to create that moral compass. These are the beliefs, doctrines, and laws that govern that individual's choices. When all of these overlap with that individual's personality, their character is formed, and whenever you see character, you will find characteristics. Our characteristics are the individual expressions of who we are as a whole. They include both our strengths and weaknesses and everything that makes us who we are.

Anointing: Our anointing is the merging of God's Spirit with our own. It is the call, the grace, the ability and the power that rests on our lives. All of these come together to aid us in

75

the fulfillment of our assignments in the Earth. In Luke 4:18-19, Jesus went on record with these words, "The Spirit of the Lord is upon me, because he hath anointed me to preach the gospel to the poor; he hath sent me to heal the brokenhearted, to preach deliverance to the captives, and recovering of sight to the blind, to set at liberty them that are bruised, to preach the acceptable year of the Lord." To get a better understanding of this, let's look at the moment when Jehu was anointed king over Israel. 2 Kings 9:1-3 tells the story; it reads, "And Elisha the prophet called one of the children of the prophets, and said unto him, Gird up thy loins, and take this box of oil in thine hand, and go to Ramothgilead: And when thou comest thither, look out there Jehu the son of Jehoshaphat the son of Nimshi, and go in, and make him arise up from among his brethren, and carry him to an inner chamber; then take the box of oil, and pour it on his head, and say, Thus saith the LORD, I have anointed thee king over Israel. Then open the door, and flee, and tarry not." Please note that the primary reason for physically anointing a king was to notify everyone around that the individual was holy or set apart for a specific function. When Jehu emerged from the room, the other soldiers that had been with him could clearly see the oil running down his face. Let's look at the rest of that story. 2 Kings 9:4-10 reads, "So the young man, even the young man the prophet, went to Ramothgilead. And when he came, behold, the captains of the host were sitting; and he said, I have an errand to thee, O captain. And Jehu said, Unto which of all us? And he said, To thee, O captain. And he arose, and went into the house; and he poured the oil on his head, and said unto him, Thus saith the LORD God of Israel, I have anointed thee king over the people of the LORD, even over Israel. And thou shalt smite the house of Ahab thy master, that I may avenge the blood of my servants the prophets, and the blood of all the servants of the LORD, at the hand of Jezebel. For the whole house of Ahab shall perish: and I will cut off from Ahab him that pisseth against the wall, and him that is shut up and left in Israel: And I will make the house of Ahab like the house of Jeroboam the son of Nebat, and like the house of Baasha the son of Ahijah: And the dogs shall eat Jezebel in the portion of Jezreel, and there shall be none to bury her. And he opened the door, and fled." Notice that with the anointing, came a set of words. Remember what a spirit is! It is comprised of words! This was Jehu's assignment! Jehu had that same assignment since birth, but at that moment, he was empowered or legalized to carry out that assignment.

Assignment: Your assignment is the reason in which you were born or whatever task that you were elected to accept. Esther was born to be queen, however, Esau forfeited his inheritance or assignment for a bowl of soul. He sold it to his brother! Jewish tradition, at that time, dictated that the eldest son of a man would receive the equivalent of that man's spirit. The eldest child would receive a double portion. Esau didn't respect his father's mantle; this is a common issue we see today, whereas anointed people make the mistake of ranking their carnality (fleshly desires) over their identities and assignments. And because of this, many believers are overlooked, stagnated and rejected by God to complete those assignments. In Hosea 4:6, the Lord said, "My people are destroyed for lack of knowledge: because thou hast rejected knowledge, I will also reject thee, that thou shalt be no priest to me: seeing thou hast forgotten the law of thy God, I will also forget thy children." This means that the individuals in question have an assignment, but God has taken back their assignments. Why? Because they rejected knowledge, which is the foundational level of an anointing. And please note that many are called, but few are chosen (see Matthew 22:14). What this means is, many people have assignments; many people are anointed to carry out specific functions, but only a few are chosen or, better yet, placed in position and empowered to fulfill the calls on their lives. This is because, again, many people reject knowledge. They don't want to come to Bible study or even read their Bibles at home. They don't want to sit in church too long. They don't want to learn about Kingdom principles or even learn about YAHWEH. They just want to go to Heaven.

Remember, you were created to create. Your assignment is to destroy the works of the enemy. Now, the means in which you do this is called talents. We'll discuss this a little later.

The Seasons of a Gift

Ecclesiastes 3:1-8 reads, "To every thing there is a season, and a time to every purpose under the heaven: A time to be born, and a time to die; a time to plant, and a time to pluck up that which is planted; a time to kill, and a time to heal; a time to break down, and a time to build up; a time to weep, and a time to laugh; a time to mourn, and a time to dance; a time to cast away stones, and a time to gather stones together; a time to embrace, and a time to refrain from embracing; a time to get, and a time to lose; a time to keep, and a time to cast away; a time to rend, and a time to sew; a time to keep silence, and a time to speak; a time to love, and a time to hate; a time of war, and a time of peace." In short, there is a time for everything. This means that we can be out of season and inside the constraints of a season. Think of the four seasons of the year. They are Winter, Spring, Summer and Fall. Each season has weather patterns; these are all similar to what we refer to as characteristics. The Winter season is often marked by extremely cold weather, snow and rather gloomy days. The Spring season is often marked by rainy weather, some sunshine, some relatively chilly days and the emergence of flowers. The summer season is marked by extremely warm weather, the presence of certain plants and fruits and longer days. The fall season is often characterized by relatively warm days that get windier as we approach the winter, the dying of certain plants, the falling away of leaves, along with the bright yellow, orange and red colors of the leaves that fall to the ground. And when we see these changes taking place, we all begin to shuffle through our wardrobes so that we can prepare for the seasons that we are entering.

Every gift not only has a season, but every gift is a season. What this means is the presence of a gift is often characterized by certain changes. When Daniel arrived in Babylon, all of a sudden, there was someone present to interpret the king's dreams. This undoubtedly made King Nebuchadnezzar a happier man. As the scriptures note, the pagan king even began to worship the Most High God. So, when a gift arrives in his or her time, a change is inevitable. It is also noticeable. It causes everyone within a certain proximity of that gift to have to adjust to that gift's arrival. This is what it means to shift atmospheres. A gift should never submit to an atmosphere that's antithetical to the God he or she serves. Instead, a gift must bring Heaven to Earth wheresoever he or she goes. This is why the men wanted to kill Daniel. His arrival meant that they wouldn't be used, called upon or reverenced as much as they once had been. Why is this important? It's simple. As a gift, you must understand that the minute you are placed in a system that once thrived without you, there will be a marked change in that system, and it will upset some of the people who were once celebrated within that system. This is because it marks the end of their seasons. This doesn't necessarily mean that they won't be needed or used, but it does mean that they won't be needed as much as they once were or used as much as they once were. We see this in every organization, business or establishment. The progenitors or firstlings of that particular organization are oftentimes the ones who cause the most damage to that organization in the end because it's hard for them to watch the systems that they've built begin to expire when new systems and new gifts begin to emerge. But that's the thing. In order for an organism or an organization to survive, it must change! Old systems will pass away and new seasons will emerge. All the same, those new systems will eventually grow old and expire, and newer systems, technologies and gifts will arise. But if you want to elongate or extend your seasons in the spotlight, you have to be willing to grow and change with the times. This means that you have to be always learning and abounding, not just in the things of God, but in natural knowledge. To better grasp this, we must understand what exactly a season is.

The Greek word for "season" is "kairos." It is also the Greek word for "time." According to Strong's Concordance, it means "fitting season, season, opportunity, occasion, time." Consider the life of Moses. For forty years, he was gifted, but he wasn't necessarily a gift. He was a Jewish man living in an Egyptian castle while his Jewish brethren served as slaves. Can you imagine the jealousy that surrounded him? The Jews likely saw him as a spoiled, entitled and weak traitor. The Egyptians likely saw him as a nobody who'd lucked up and found himself in the castle because of Pharaoh's rich and spoiled daughter. This means that it is possible that Moses dealt majorly with rejection because he couldn't find anyone to relate to. This means that he also didn't have anyone to look up to. Howbeit, Moses would go on to kill an Egyptian man after he found the Egyptian harassing a Jew, the news of his crime would be made public, and Moses would go on the run to Midian. There, he would spend the next forty years in hiding. This means that his gift wasn't needed for the first forty years of his life. But then, a calendared event was scheduled to take place. The cries of God's people would reach up to Him, and He needed a savior (of sorts) to assist Him in saving the Jews. This is when Moses found himself feeling compelled to return to Egypt. At the time, his life was going well. He had a wife, a decent father-in-law, a job and most of all, he had stability. Nevertheless, he also had a gift, and that gift, if left alone, would have brought him great misery. When we bury a gift or a talent, it begins to decompose. The stench of this decomposition is what we often refer to as depression (in some cases). Depression can take over the moment a gift is activated outside of his or her purpose, meaning the individual is not in the right position to use his or her gift. This is like cranking up a car in the middle of a desert. The car needs lanes and fuel, and the driver needs signs, directions and an overall destination. If you toss a man in the middle of a desert, hand him a set of car keys and you don't tell him where to go, he will go in circles until he runs out of fuel. He will experience frustration, fear, hopelessness, and depression because he has a vehicle (way to accomplish an assignment) but no direction (instructions or means to accomplish that assignment).

Why Opposition is Needed

Think of a spectrum. Remember, on each side of a spectrum is something that is antithetical to whatever it is that rests on the opposite end of that spectrum. In the middle of that spectrum, we find creatures that have will or, better yet, the ability to make a choice. Each creature has a purpose. Each creature has an assignment. Each creature has a set of skills and abilities that were installed or implanted within it that are designed to help that creature accomplish its purpose. But it is only within the will of God that each creature's purpose is manifested. The will of God is the garden of God that our spirits feed on. If we eat any other diet, what we've eaten will begin to eat us from the inside out. All the same, each direction on that spectrum has weather patterns. All too often, the direction that is contradictory to the creature's purpose has the most favorable weather conditions, but again, our gifts only work in climates, environments and situations that are unfavorable. This means that the wrong way feels better, but ultimately, it renders the gift or the gifted individual weak and powerless. This works against the mental health of the gift because we grow our strength when we have something that is opposing or resisting us. This gives us purpose; this gives us something to use our gift on. Think about a bodybuilder. In order for the bodybuilder to build muscle, he needs weights. He needs forces that work against his body. He has to apply pressure if he wants to get stronger, but if everything that's handed to him is lightweight and easy to carry, he cannot and will not get stronger, nor will he build his stamina. Consequently, while his life would be easier for a season, he would not be able to persevere when the seasons changed. It's inevitable! At some point, he will need to lift something, to carry something, to push something, to resist something or to overcome something, but if life has always been easy for him, he won't have the mental or the physical strength needed to persevere or survive. Can you see why God allowed you to go through many of the storms you've endured? God gives the greatest tests of life to the people He's called to the highest platforms. Most of them won't make it to the top of their perspective mountains, however. This is because most people don't focus on the fact that they are creatures with an assignment. Instead, they get distracted by other people, and they begin to compare and then complain about their results or realities. Hear me—if your life was arduous, you are in a more coveted position than someone who's had an easy life, even though you may not realize this just yet! You have strength, wisdom, experience and sustenance that they do not possess! What would annoy you would crush them! This is why they envy you! This is why they hate you! This is why, try as they may, they cannot get you off of their minds! Do you understand how weak a man must be in order for him to be unable to stop thinking about another human being?! How sick were those men who found themselves obsessed with Daniel and his success?! This is the very definition of insanity!

THE 4 SEASONS
OF A GIFT

"While the earth remaineth, seedtime and harvest, and cold and heat, and summer and winter, and day and night shall not cease."   Genesis 8:22

LIGHT SHINES THE BRIGHTEST

DEVELOPMENT

SUMMER MOST VISIBLE

DISCOVERY

SPRING

MARK 4:28

100

60

30

FALL

DEPLOYMENT

WINTER DARKNESS

CAVE SEASON   YOUR JOB IS TO SURVIVE

TIME TO GO BACK INTO THE CAVE

BENEATH THE SURFACE

TIME OF HIBERNATION

THINGS BEGIN TO DIE OUT

@PICTUREITPOSSIBLE

A Gift for a Season and a Season for a Gift

Consider the life of Esther. One day, she got the news that both her parents had been killed. Can you imagine her pain? Can you imagine how difficult it was for her to find herself living with her cousin, Mordecai? But, you see, God didn't want Esther to be weak-minded. She needed the ability to shift from one extreme to another in little to no time. Other women could have and would have become suicidal. But Esther walked into the castle for the first time, and while she may have experienced fear and while she may have experienced anxiety, these feelings were not new to her. She knew that she would survive them, after all, nothing could be worse than what she'd experienced when she'd lost her parents. Esther was a gift. She was not only gifted, but she was a gift. And while King Xerxes may have felt like she was his gift, in truth, she was a gift to God's people, and most of all, she was a gift to God. You see, God is Alpha (the Beginning) and Omega (the End). He knows everything that will happen in between! He knew that Haman would arise and plot the destruction of the Jews. For every demonic twist and turn that Satan has devised, God has always been a million light years ahead of him! He has always birthed gifts into this Earth to confront and eradicate demonic systems. These gifts all too often didn't have the best upbringings. They were raised in broken families; they were rejected, molested, raped, abandoned, persecuted and left for dead. They were forgotten about, laughed at, underestimated and discounted. Did it affect their mental health? Yes, it did! But many of these gifts continued to survive and thrive in the harshest climates, that is until their seasons arrived. And without warning, they were thrust into uncomfortable environments and situations, but this was not something that was new to them! This is where their gifts began to activate all the more. They experienced the winds of opposition coming at them from many directions, but get this—it didn't move them because they were used to it! It didn't phase them the way people thought it would phase them! They had been broken, beaten and rejected for such a time as this!

Esther would go on to save God's people, and like many gifts before and after her, when her season, her moment or her assignment was completed, she simply faded off of our radars. She didn't cease to exist. Her life may have become "normal" or better than normal after everything was said and done. This means that while there is a time for your gift to be highlighted, celebrated and used, there is also a season of rest. This is the time when another gift will arise to relieve you. This is not the time to compete with that gift, to sabotage that gift or to allow yourself to feel incompetent. This is the time when you should be reaping the benefits of your yes to God.

Let's look at two stories. John 2:2-5 reads, "And both Jesus was called, and his disciples, to the marriage. And when they wanted wine, the mother of Jesus saith unto him, They have no wine. Jesus saith unto her, Woman, what have I to do with thee? Mine hour is not yet come." John 7:1-6 reads, "After these things Jesus walked in Galilee: for he would not walk in Jewry, because the Jews sought to kill him. Now the Jews' feast of tabernacles was at hand. His brethren therefore said unto him, Depart hence, and go into Judaea, that thy disciples also may see the works that thou doest. For there is no man that doeth any thing in secret, and he himself seeketh to be known openly. If thou do these things, shew thyself to the world. For neither did his brethren believe in him. Then Jesus said unto them, My time is not yet come: but your time is alway ready." Notice in both of these stories, we find Jesus talking about time. He understood that there was a time for His gift to be utilized. He didn't necessarily want to perform miracles at the wedding festival because He understood that performing miracles would draw attention to Him. Joseph, in his immaturity, did not understand this precept. He'd had a couple of dreams, and instead of keeping them to himself, he'd rushed over to tell his brothers and his father. Did he think they'd be excited for him? Not at all. Joseph had history with his brothers. Let's not think for one moment that Joseph was ignorant of their jealousy. He was likely behaving like a child does. He was likely mocking his brothers. This set the stage for the events that would follow. Joseph would be sold into slavery, lied on, tossed into prison and eventually find himself standing before Pharaoh interpreting his dreams. What Jesus is teaching us here is that, while we may be gifted, anointed and appointed to carry out a certain assignment, there is a time for us to be hidden, just as there is a time for us to be recognized. Most prophets who are currently in mental institutions are prophets who revealed themselves before their time! Most apostles who have chosen to use their gifts for the kingdom of darkness ended up in those positions because they revealed themselves before their time. I see it all the time! As a pastor, I have one of the most difficult jobs in the world! I have to watch gifts emerge and then crash because of their impatience. They recognize the fact that they're gifted, but they do not understand the concept of seasons. Because of this, many gifts begin to chase after microphones, cameras and platforms, hoping to reveal what God, Himself is trying to hide. They are oftentimes in the sanctuary being trained to yield their gifts to the Holy Spirit and not to emotionalism, but it is their emotions that drive them out of the church and into the darkest spotlights. And it is there that we watch their lights fade because they are attempting to shine when their gift has not been called upon. It is a hard thing to be gifted and not needed, especially when you can see needs all around you! It's like going into a restaurant and being told that there is a 30-minute wait when you can clearly see open tables and booths. Howbeit, the problem is, they don't have someone to when saw the voidsman or cover those tables. Just remember that for everything and every gift, there is a season. And outside of its perspective season, that thing and that gift is not strong enough or bright enough to accomplish the assignment that God has for him or her. Outside of Esther's season, she was not ready to go before King Xerxes. Like any other child, Esther likely had a season of immaturity. She had a season when she felt like she was right and nobody understood her. Joseph's immaturity was placed on display for the whole world to see and it cost him dearly. Jesus, on the other hand, understood that it wasn't His time, and He wasn't willing to allow His gifts to be exploited before their time.

The Four Seasons of a Gift

"While the earth remaineth, seedtime and harvest, and cold and heat, and summer and winter, and day and night shall not cease" (Genesis 8:22). The four seasons of the Earth correspond to the four seasons that every gift endures.

Winter	Spring	Summer	Fall

- **Winter:** Season of Darkness
- **Spring:** Season of Discovery
- **Summer:** Season of Development
- **Fall:** Season of Deployment

Winter

God is more than a gift. He gave Himself to us freely, and this makes Him a gift to us, but He is so much more than that. It's impossible to confine who He is or describe who He is using a single word, so we can just say that He's good since good is an adjective that describes how He is and everything that He does. The Bible refers to Him as Light. Merriam-Webster defines light as "the bright form of energy given off by something (as the sun) that makes it possible to see." Light is a form of energy, and energy (in physics) simply means the ability (or capacity) to do work. Going back to Genesis 1, we find God in action. "In the beginning God created the heaven and the earth. And the earth was without form, and void; and darkness was upon the face of the deep. And the Spirit of God moved upon the face of the waters" (Genesis 1:1-2). What did Jesus do when He saw the voids and the darkness? He moved. What was He doing? He was creating energy. He'd discovered an empty space, so He decided to fill it. If we had been physically present on the Earth before God moved upon it, we would have frozen to death. The Earth was in a winter-like state, and this is why it was dark.

Every gift or creative must endure the Winter of his or her gifting. This is the season of darkness, the season of obscurity and the season when the gift has not produced enough to fill the voids in a particular space. Then again, the individual may have produced a lot of materials or performed at a lot of events, however, no one knows too much about this individual because:

1. The individual's skill level has not yet reached its peak, but is instead in a stage of infancy. Think of a graphic designer. They're all created equally, but they aren't all equally talented. Joey may have created one hundred flyers, but this does not mean that he's good at what he does. First and foremost, we must ask the question: is Joey on the right side of the mountain? And if he is, he still needs more training, development and mentorship before his name becomes largely recognized in that specific industry or world.

2. The individual's character does not match his or her level of skill. There are people who are incredibly good at what they do, but they have bad attitudes, they are unreliable or they are unpredictable, meaning you may get excellent work from them one day, but the next day, they will throw something together.

3. The individual has a bad reputation. This typically happens when people try to ascend on the wrong side of the mountain, and again, they become villainous on the other sides of the mountains. They are then reputed to lie, cheat and steal in their attempts to get to the top. This doesn't necessarily mean that the person is bad; it simply means that if you put the right gift in the wrong industry, that gift's character will begin to break down until the gift becomes good at what he or she does, but wicked in his or her ways. We meet them all the time. People who are gifted, meaning they've paired an education with their gifting, but their character repels people from working with them.

Every creative has to endure the Winter. This is a time of hibernation, a time of rest and a time of self-development. This is the cave season; this is the time when the gift has to intentionally withdraw himself or herself from others to heal, to be restored and most of all, to pray. If you're in this season, your job is to survive it.

THE 4 SEASONS
OF A GIFT

"While the earth remaineth, seedtime and harvest, and cold and heat, and summer and winter, and day and night shall not cease."   Genesis 8:22

LIGHT SHINES THE BRIGHTEST

DEVELOPMENT

SUMMER — MOST VISIBLE

DISCOVERY

SPRING

MARK 4:28

100
60
30

FALL

DEPLOYMENT

WINTER — DARKNESS

YOUR JOB IS TO SURVIVE

CAVE SEASON

TIME TO GO BACK INTO THE CAVE

BENEATH THE SURFACE

TIME OF HIBERNATION

THINGS BEGIN TO DIE OUT

Every gift goes through cycles and seasons.
At some point it's going to
TURN.

Spring

The dark days are over, but the individual is not in his or her finest hour just yet! Mark 4:28 says, "For the earth bringeth forth fruit of herself; first the blade, then the ear, after that the full corn in the ear." This is the season when the gift breaks the ground of his or her potential. The gift is not ready to bear fruit just yet! In this hour, the individual must be intentional about getting developed. What types of fruit are beginning to spring up? Are there any barren spaces? If so, what happened?

This is when the individual begins to discover his or her talents, and the level of his or her ability. This can be an exciting time or one of disappointment. This is when we plant the most seeds, meaning we have to be intentional and strategic about who we are around. Proverbs 6:6-8 reads, "Go to the ant, thou sluggard; consider her ways, and be wise: Which having no guide, overseer, or ruler, provideth her meat in the summer, and gathereth her food in the harvest." This scripture is talking about mentorship and development. Please note that a sluggard is a person who is habitually lazy. Of course, they are being compared with slugs which, of course, are slow, snail-like creatures that feed on the harvests of farmers, meaning they are pests. In this, God correlates an ant with a wise and diligent person who is in the Summer of his or her gifting. So, in short, this scripture can be translated as saying, "Those of you who are lazy, go and find yourself a mentor who is diligent and fruitful, but don't just go there to eat up what they've produced.

Consider their ways or, better yet, learn their ways." This is what you do in your Spring season. You need someone to be accountable to, someone to give you language to the many things you will experience or have experienced. Without this language, you are left on your own to interpret these experiences, and this will always end in you misunderstanding or misdiagnosing a moment, which means that you'll miss the moment and have to repeat it!

Summer

This is the season when a gift shines its brightest! This is the season of breakthrough! In this season, you have your greatest measure of visibility! Your name has grown, and you are now recognized because of your unique skill-sets or abilities.

During the Summer, everything that started blossoming during the Winter is now in full bloom! At the same time, the sun is at its hottest, so you have to strategically pull yourself away so that you don't burn out because this is your busiest season! And finally, during the Summer, the fruits from most trees are at their ripest! But one of the problems that can and does occur in this season is, we can easily begin to feel intimidated by our own gifts. When this happens, the farmer does not take what he's produced to the market, but instead allows it to rot! He takes a few pictures of it to share on his social media, but after that, those fruits become the equivalent of dung! Hear me—every farmer knows that he has to:

1. Promote what he does!
2. Sell what he's created!
3. Give to the needy!

And this is mostly done in the Summer! In short, this is our favorite season, but we have to make the best of it because it will determine what our next four seasons look like!

Fall

This is the season of deployment. In the Fall season, the plants and the fruits begin to break down, but this isn't entirely bad because they begin to create the fertilizer needed for next year's harvest. This is the season when the gift must begin to retreat to his or her cave in preparation for the Winter. This reminds me of two well-known fables:

1. "A Wild Boar was sharpening his tusks busily against the stump of a tree, when a Fox happened by. Now the Fox was always looking for a chance to make fun of his neighbors. So he made a great show of looking anxiously about, as if in fear of some hidden enemy. But the Boar kept right on with his work. 'Why are you doing that?' asked the Fox at last with a grin. 'There isn't any danger that I can see.' 'True enough,' replied the Boar, 'but when danger does come there will not be time for such work as this. My weapons will have to be ready for use then, or I shall suffer for it.'" (Source: The Wild Boar and the Fox/Milo Winter).

2. "A commonwealth of ants, having, after a busy summer, provided everything for their wants in the

winter, were about shutting themselves up for that dreary season, when a grasshopper in great distress, and in dread of perishing with cold and hunger, approached their avenues, and with great humility begged they would relieve his wants, and permit him to take shelter in any corner of their comfortable mansion. One of the ants asked him how he had disposed of his time in summer, that he had not taken pains and laid in a stock, as they had done? Alas! my friends, says he, I passed away the time merrily and pleasantly, in drinking, singing, and dancing, and never once thought of winter. If that be the case, replied the ant, all I have to say is this: that they who drink, sing, and dance in the summer, run a great risk of starving in the winter." (Source: Fables of Aesop/The Ant and the Grasshopper/Thomas Bewick).

The moral of both fables is be prepared! Fall is the season that gives us just enough heat and just enough coolness to transition from the Winter to the Summer, which are both extremes. Fall is a middle-ground; it warns us of the impending Winter so that we can utilize that time to buy ourselves some winter clothes, make sure that our heaters are working, change the tires on our cars (if we live in the North) and stock up on everything we will need to remain both safe and comfortable. The same is true when it comes to our skills and abilities. Think about a man who does lawn care. The Summer months are his most lucrative months, and the same can be said of most of the Fall. When he sees fallen leaves, when he notices that the grass isn't growing to its full capacity and when he notices the brown patches of grass, he knows that he has to find another way to make money. He may take to raking leaves, but people don't usually require this service every two weeks, so he has to have another set of skills to benefit from. Howbeit, he must use the Fall season to transition between both gifts and he must use this season to withdraw himself from the people he worked for.

In truth, it could be said that both Fall and Spring are transitional seasons that notify us of the impending Summers or Falls. We get to enjoy all seasons, however, when it comes to gifting, it is important that we recognize what season we're in, make sure that we're adequately prepared for and supplied in that season, and most importantly, we have to always make sure that we're ready for the next extreme. This is why Joseph was needed to interpret Pharaoh's dreams. God was warning Pharaoh through his dreams to prepare himself and the people for a famine.

- **Pharaoh's Dream** (Genesis 41:15-24): And Pharaoh said unto Joseph, I have dreamed a dream, and there is none that can interpret it: and I have heard say of thee, that thou canst understand a dream to interpret it. And Joseph answered Pharaoh, saying, It is not in me: God shall give Pharaoh an answer of peace. And Pharaoh said unto Joseph, In my dream, behold, I stood upon the bank of the river: And, behold, there came up out of the river seven kine, fatfleshed and well favoured; and they fed in a meadow: And, behold, seven other kine came up after them, poor and very ill favoured and leanfleshed, such as I never saw in all the land of Egypt for badness: And the lean and the ill favoured kine did eat up the first seven fat kine: And when they had eaten them up, it could not be known that they had eaten them; but they were still ill favoured, as at the beginning. So I awoke. And I saw in my dream, and, behold, seven ears came up in one stalk, full and good: And, behold, seven ears, withered, thin, and blasted with the east wind, sprung up after them: And the thin ears devoured the seven good ears: and I told this unto the magicians; but there was none that could declare it to me.

- **Joseph's Interpretation** (Genesis 41:25-36): And Joseph said unto Pharaoh, The dream of Pharaoh is one: God hath shewed Pharaoh what he is about to do. The seven good kine are seven years; and the seven good ears are seven years: the dream is one. And the seven thin and ill favoured kine that came up after them are seven years; and the seven empty ears blasted with the east wind shall be seven years of famine. This is the thing which I have spoken unto Pharaoh: What God is about to do he sheweth unto Pharaoh. Behold, there come seven years of great plenty throughout all the land of Egypt: And there shall arise after them seven years of famine; and all the plenty shall be forgotten in the land of Egypt; and the famine shall consume the land; And the plenty shall not be known in the land by reason of that famine following; for it shall be very grievous. And for that the dream was doubled unto Pharaoh twice; it is because the thing is established by God, and God will shortly bring it to pass. Now therefore let Pharaoh look out a man discreet and wise, and set him over the land of Egypt. Let Pharaoh do this, and let him appoint officers over the land, and take up the fifth part of the land of Egypt in the seven plenteous years. And let them gather all the food of those good years that come, and lay up corn under the hand of Pharaoh, and let them keep food in the cities. And that food shall be for store to the land against the seven years of famine, which shall be in the land of Egypt; that the land perish not through the famine.

"When all the world appears to be in a tumult, and nature itself is feeling the assault of climate change, the seasons retain their essential rhythm. Yes, fall gives us a premonition of winter, but then, winter, will be forced to relent, once again, to the new beginnings of soft greens, longer light, and the sweet air of spring."

Madeleine M. Kunin

The Mind of a Gift

What happened to you is the past, what's happening through you is the present, and what happens because of you is the future. All the same, the past happened to you, for you and through you; the same is true for the present and will be present in the future. This is because we have existed, we are existing and we will exist in the three dimensions of time. And each interval brings with it the tools, the revelation and the people we need to accomplish whatever it is that we are set to accomplish during those times. Consider Joseph's climatic moment. In this, we find Joseph at the height of his potential. He has served as the second most powerful man in charge of Egypt, he has interpreted many of Pharaoh's dreams, he has found his family, and now, he has the opportunity to reveal to his brothers just who he truly was. Purpose fulfilled, Joseph was in a space where he felt untouchable. His brothers couldn't harm him anymore, and everything that he'd dreamed of happening had already taken place. What happens when the prophecies finally come to pass? What happens to the human soul when we have finished our assignments here in the Earth? Do we immediately pass away? In Joseph's case, we see that Joseph was able to make amends with his brothers. This was his moment. He could revisit the past and allow unforgiveness to discount everything he'd worked so hard for, or he could simply forgive his brothers and move on with his life. In that very present moment, he decided to forgive.

His choice would have directly impacted his future because it is possible to serve God your entire life, accomplish whatever it is that you've set out to accomplish, and completely diminish it all simply by living in the past. This impacts our mental health and our physical well-being. All the same, anything that influences the mind has the ability to shape our futures.

God exists outside of the three dimensions of time, which again are past, present and future. This means that He is eternal. Remember, outside of the spectrum of life, there exists eternity. As humans, we are eternal creatures because we are spirits that live in a body.

Body	Soul	Spirit
30-Fold	60-Fold	100-Fold
Past	Present	Future

The body, also known as the flesh, corresponds to the past, even though it is present. This is because the body has memory, and every craving we have, every temptation we experience and every decision that we make is directly connected to whatever it is that we've consumed, both mentally and physically. The soul, on the other hand, is connected to our present since it is what we use to make decisions for today and for our futures. The soul does not have the ability to change the past. It can only shape the present. The shape of our present will determine the shape and state of our future. And finally, there is our spirit. Our spirit is connected to our future because it is the eternal part of us. The decisions that we make with our souls (mind, will and emotions) will determine which side of eternity we live on and what we will experience in this event called life. It is possible to be saved and miserable, meaning we can be presently frustrated, miserable and suicidal, all the while awaiting an eternity with God. This is why the Bible says in Matthew 15:26, "For what is a man profited, if he shall gain the whole world, and lose his own soul? Or what shall a man give in exchange for his soul?" Please note that we've been reading this scripture wrong for many years. We've misinterpreted it to mean that some people will chase after the wealth of the Earth, only to find themselves in eternal damnation, and while this is true, this isn't exactly what the scripture meant. Again, the soul is comprised of the mind, will and emotions. In this, God isn't just talking about the future of a man, but also the conditions of his present. We see it all the time, even in the church. Many people lose their peace or their sanity simply because they keep chasing after lifestyles that are contrary to their makeup. This is what it means to be double-minded, and according to the scriptures, a double-minded man is unstable in all his ways (see James 1:8). In this, the Bible is talking about mental instability.

Three Compartments of the Soul		
Mind	Will	Emotions

The Three Dimension of the Mind		
Conscious	Subconscious	Unconscious

Consider an apple. It has three layers to it. First, there is the skin of the apple. This is the protective coating. We can relate this to our conscious mind. Next, there is the flesh of the apple. This is the interior, flesh or part of the apple that we eat. We can relate this to the subconscious. And finally, at the core of the apple, we will find the seeds. This allows the apple to reproduce itself or to exist in the future. And of course, we can relate this to the unconscious mind.

Remember that you are a gift, and as such, there is a time for your gifting to be revealed to and used by God. Howbeit, you are like an apple. The apple, before its time, is small; it has not reached its full potential. How do we know when an apple is mature or ripe? The following information was taken from PickYourOwn.com:

1. **Days from bloom:** The most accurate method is to count the number of days since the tree bloomed in the Spring. Each variety of apple has a specific number of days to reach its optimum ripeness. Of course, that can vary, based on weather conditions, but it's pretty accurate. But if you do know or remember the date the trees bloomed, here are the other ways to tell when to harvest the apples:

2. **Color.** Color, both on the outside and the flesh, is a useful indication of maturity. Depending on the variety, apples may be yellow, red, green or combinations of these colors at harvest. When the green has almost completely given way to yellow, a yellow variety is mature. With red blush or striped apples, the area

where there is no red color usually changes from green to yellowish at maturity. Some of the newer red strains are challenging because they are red all over long before they are sweet and mature. In these, the change in the color of the flesh goes from greenish to white when they are ripe. Red Delicious spur-types apples are odd in that the greenish tint may take months in storage to disappear, but they are fine to eat before that!

3. **Ease of separation.** Unless the orchardist has used a "stop-drop" spray that causes the apples to stay on the tree, mature apples are separated easily from the tree by twisting it upward in a rotating motion.

4. **Seeds:** Cut a sample apple horizontally and look at the seeds. Usually, the seeds become brown when the fruit is ripe. That's more true with later ripening varieties, like Fuji. With early season apple varieties, like Gala, they may be ready to eat before the seeds turn brown.

5. **Fruit drop.** When a few good, healthy apples drop to the ground, the apples on the tree are nearly mature. (rotten, buggy or diseased apples can drop at any time)

6. **Softness and flavor.** The taste test never fails! When an apple becomes slightly softer and tastes sweet and juicy, it is mature. Some varieties, such as Delicious, become sweeter in storage; but that's different from ripening.

7. **The Iodine starch test.** An apple is cut horizontally through the core and sprayed with a mild iodine solution. Since the iodine turns the cells containing starch dark, unripe apples turn dark, ripe apples remain white.

(Source: PickYourOwn.com/Apple Ripeness: How to tell when apples are ripe and ready to pick from your apple trees)

An apple picked out of season is edible, but it is oftentimes bitter. An apple that is left on the tree too long will become rotten to its core. So, an apple needs the right amount of exposure to the sun, water and time before it is ready to be picked. If it is not picked before its time, it could potentially waste away. The same is true for you. Your mental health is important to God, but your anxiousness is not. This is because Satan tempts you to come outside of God's timing, just like he tempted Eve to step outside of God's will. That's just what he does. He attacks a gift in two of his or her most delicate moments.

1. **When the gift does not yet know who he or she is.** When you were a child, you had no clue as to who you were. And if you existed outside of the church, you didn't know who God is as well. So, you studied everyone around you in your attempt to find yourself or to create a version of yourself that would be acceptable to the people you loved and esteemed the most. That's when you were introduced to a television set, and on the big screen of your television, you saw

men and women who embodied excellence. They were attractive, intelligent and they appeared to be more than happy. In this never-ending lineup of faces, you found a few personalities that you wanted to channel. These personalities took you further and further away from your authentic identity.

2. **When the gift begins to recognize his or her potential.** Think of a child who's discovered his sexual organs for the first time. He's an infant, but he doesn't understand how delicate those parts of his body are, so anytime his diaper comes off, he takes his hand and begins to mess with his potential. His parents or whomever it is that is changing his diaper will remove his hand because that person knows that the child could hurt himself and completely destroy his own potential or future. Howbeit, when that child becomes a teenager, he experiences another rediscovery regarding that area of his body. At this moment, his hormones begin to arise, his voice deepens and he begins to think that he is man enough to make his own decisions. This is especially true if he's engaged in sexual activity. It is during this time when this young man will be in his most rebellious stage. All of this is due to the discovery of a member or a part of his body! In this, he doesn't yet recognize his full potential.

The parents of that young man in question could move aside and let him have his way. They could allow him to be controlled by his inexperience, his hormones and his emotions. But if they did this, they wouldn't be great parents (or even good parents, for that matter). They would be enablers. What would then happen is that young man would find himself tossed to and fro by his feelings, by peer pressure and by the many forces or winds that come his way. He would likely find himself fathering children with several women, getting into drugs and completely making a mess of his life. But during this sensitive moment of his life, his parents have to put the greatest amount of pressure on him. It is during this time when his parents appear to be the cruelest because he is being driven by his maturity. Moving completely out of his way would be the equivalent of turning him over to a reprobate mind. It would mean that his parents allowed him to do whatever it is that he wanted to do at the expense of his mental health, his emotional health and his future. Now, do you understand why God doesn't give you what you want when you want it? You may even be "good enough" to have whatever it is that you've been praying for, and while this is admirable, God looks at the texture of your soul. If your mind, will and emotions are too soft, whatever it is that you're asking for may pierce you to no ends. Meaning, it could cause you to be exposed to the elements of this world. Imagine a fork piercing an apple before its time, and that apple is resting at the top of a tree. What do you think would happen to it? The weather would cause the apple to begin to rot. All the same, insects would make their way into the apple and begin to eat away at its core. That particular apple would never mature. It would be consumed before its time. Going back to Joseph, imagine what his life would have been like had he gone before Pharaoh before his time. Let's go back even further! Could you imagine what would have happened if Potiphar's wife had attempted to seduce Joseph when he was still in the season of discovery? Do you know how many gifts throw away their futures because of sex, power, unforgiveness and impatience?!

The body, once again, represents the 30-fold dimension. Every gift must first overcome his or her flesh before that gift can move into the next dimension or season. Please note that a dimension, according to Oxford Languages, is "a measurable extent of some kind, such as length, breadth, depth, or height." This means that when we are dealing with the mind, God measures us by our choices, since what we do and do not do; yes, even what we procrastinate on doing reveals the state of our minds. The soul, on the other hand, represents the 60-fold dimension. Every gift must learn to manage his or her own mind. The mind is like a garden. It has to be pruned, some form of repellent has to be utilized, it has to be watered and it has to be tended to regularly. Consider the Garden of Eden. Adam had been given the assignment to keep the grounds, however, Satan managed to creep into the garden. Gardens represent places of order, whereas wildernesses represent places of disorder. Satan tempted Eve and managed to get her in disorder. Please note that the word "disorder" is what psychiatrists today use to describe the diseases of the mind. Eve's mind had been exposed to something that it was not supposed to be exposed to, and consequently, Eve tempted her husband, and they both ended up on the wrong side of God's will. They both ended up in an agreement with the kingdom of darkness, which is a place of disorder. This set the stage for a new world order. All of a sudden, the couple would be evicted from the garden, and every child born to them would be born outside of God's will. This doesn't mean that they were not supposed to exist when they came into existence, it means that they were born outside of order. They were born into what we call a generational curse.

One thing that needs to be understood about a curse is that it doesn't necessarily deal with a set of events and variables that surround a person; these are the fruits of a curse. A curse means "without God's blessing." Where God's blessing doesn't exist, God's favor, grace and presence will not exist. And remember, outside of God, there is darkness, voids and everything antithetical to God's presence. This means that a curse isn't just the presence of spoken words, it is the absence of the Word Himself! This also means that a man or woman who is scheduled to step into the blessings of God can step outside the will of God and experience what it means to be accursed. Look at King Solomon! God had already blessed him before he'd ever made an adult decision because of his father, David. This is a generational blessing! God established Solomon's throne forever before Solomon sat on the throne. But what did Solomon end up doing? He stepped outside the will of God by marrying pagan women. In short, they were witches who led him into idol worship.

This means that Solomon lost his soul; that is, his mind. This led to the perverting of his emotions and the deterioration of his will.

The mind of a gift is so important and so sacred that it has to be guarded and stored in a Godly environment. This doesn't mean that you have to sit in church all day, but it does mean that the gift must be mindful of what he or she exposes his or her heart to. Proverbs 4:23 says it this way, "Above all else, guard your heart, for everything you do flows from it." Believe it or not, when the Bible references the heart, it's referencing the mind. The Greek word for "heart" is "kardia," and according to Strong's Concordance, it means "**mind, character, inner self, will, intention, center.**" But how do you guard your heart? The short answer is intentionally. The long answer is, you have to:

1. Study your Word at home on a daily basis.
2. Meditate on the Word. Meditation takes the Word from your mind to your heart.
3. Reflect on the Word. Reflection takes the Word from your heart to your mind.
4. Surround yourself with (and submit to) wise counsel.
5. Attend church weekly, including Bible Study. This keeps you from falling into the trap of "leaning to your own understanding."
6. Don't listen to music that seduces you outside the will of God.
7. Mind your eye-gates. Be mindful of what you watch on television.

8. Surround yourself with God-fearing people and people who have standards.

9. Remove your foot from evil. In other words, put space and time between yourself and toxic people. You can still share the gospel with them, but don't allow them access to your heart to make any impartations.

10. Get therapy! This helps to prune the mind of the negative, toxic and ungodly seeds that were planted when you weren't guarding your heart.

In addition to the Word of God, the mind of a creative needs the following:

1. **Information.** This doesn't have to be religious in nature. Apostle Paul said, "To the weak became I as weak, that I might gain the weak: I am made all things to all men, that I might by all means save some" (1 Corinthians 9:22). We have to go into the world's systems to save others. This means that we shouldn't just subject ourselves to everything that relates to our faith. We have traditional jobs, and we have to be in environments where unsaved people are, so we have to learn to speak their language. I'm not saying that you have to use profanity or say anything that is ungodly. I'm saying that people should be able to relate to you. In layman's terms, you need information regarding the industry or industries you are called to, and you need to learn as much as you can.

2. **Inspiration.** We are created to inspire and to be

inspired. Without inspiration, a gift loses his or her momentum. Geeks for Geeks reported the following, "Every object in the universe attracts every other object by a force which is directly proportional to product of masses of both objects and inversely proportional to square of the distance in between them. This is known as Universal Law of Gravitation. This has very interesting history and lots of handwork and research of many scientists and mathematicians" (Source: Geeks for Geeks/Newton's Universal Law of Gravitation). And while this law describes objects with mass, it is actually true in the world of spirituality. You will essentially attract people with like interests and vice versa. This is why that young girl who seems to hate dolls and everything her parents have placed in front of her suddenly comes alive when she sees her favorite ballerina on the television screen. She is what inspires her!

3. **Activation.** We all need a push from time to time, but before we receive this push, we need to be fully activated. This means that we need people in our industries or fields who outrank us to provide us with space, time, information and correction. And please note that there are two levels to activation. They are training and deployment.

And after the gift has received the adequate amount of information to at least launch his or her business, start the organization, minister to others or whatever the case may be, the gift needs a schedule! Schedules create discipline and discipline creates disciples. Without a schedule or a frequently occurring event, the gift will be gifted but will rarely use his or her gifting. This is why it's important for creatives to volunteer and work in the industries that they believe they are called to. This is because the mind of the gift has to be submerged in the world it's destined to work or serve in before its potential can emerge and be actualized. This is why Joseph had to be taken to Egypt before he could fulfill his purpose. He spent 13 years in Potiphar's house, which means that he had to learn and master the language of the Egyptians. Can you imagine how frustrating it would have been for both Pharaoh and Joseph if Joseph had a strong, unintelligible accent while attempting to interpret Pharaoh's dreams? The 13 years he spent in Potiphar's house helped him to master the Egyptian language. This is to say that God is intentional. Every world that we are catapulted in, whether we want to be there or not, is designed to prepare us for our assignments. Potiphar was likely an educated man, given the fact that he was Pharaoh's captain of the guard.

"Learning never exhausts the mind."

~Leonardo da Vinci

The Spectrum of Skill and Competence

David walked into the king's chambers. There, he saw Saul sitting on his throne. He was taller than most men; he was most intimidating. Saul's eyes pierced through the young shepherd boy. David could see hatred in his eyes. He could also see a man who was clearly being tormented by an unclean spirit. David paid his respects to the king and made his way over to the big golden lyre on the other side of the room. The room was oddly quiet, but he was about to fill it with the sweet melodies of worship. David sat down and began to play the lyre. At first, his nervousness got the best of him. What if he messed up? What if Saul hated his song selection? Nevertheless, he didn't have too much time to pacify his fears, so David touched the organ and began to stroke its strings. A beautiful sound began to emerge, and before long, Saul's eyes began to change. His fingers started moving, starting with his index finger. He tapped the arms of the throne as if he were playing the lyre himself. As David continued to play, Saul could feel the anger, the hatred and the anxiety rising up in his belly. These feelings kept rising until they reached his mouth. Saul let out a loud yawn, and just like that, he was happy again. Every tormenting spirit that had been harassing him had lifted off him. David and Saul would continue to have these sessions until the king decided to give in to his impulses. One day, he threw a javelin at David, and this would continue until David realized that it was no longer safe to go into Saul's presence.

David was a skilled man. The Bible doesn't tell us how David learned to play the lyre (also translated as harp), after all, his father, Jesse, was not a minstrel. And David wasn't just skilled at playing the harp, he was also a psalmist. Additionally, we know that David liked to dance. We don't know if he was skilled at dancing, but the Bible tells us of one incident where he'd danced before the Lord, and this had provoked his wife and Saul's daughter, Michal.

The word "competent" is defined by Oxford Languages as "having the necessary ability, knowledge, or skill to do something successfully." When dealing with the word "competent," we are often dealing with an industry or an assignment within a specific space. This particular assignment has what we refer to as requirements. If someone is able to meet those requirements, it would mean that the individual is competent. And if you know the story, David hadn't volunteered to be Saul's personal lyricist. 1 Samuel 16:14-17 reads, "But the Spirit of the LORD departed from Saul, and an evil spirit from the LORD troubled him. And Saul's servants said unto him, Behold now, an evil spirit from God troubleth thee. Let our lord now command thy servants, which are before thee, to seek out a man, who is a cunning player on an harp: and it shall come to pass, when the evil spirit from God is upon thee, that he shall play with his hand, and thou shalt be well. And Saul said unto his servants, Provide me now a man that can play well, and bring him to me." In that moment, someone immediately spoke up about David. This means that David was incredibly skilled at playing the lyre, so much so that his fame had reached some of the highest ranking individuals in the castle. 1 Samuel 16:18-19 reads, "Then answered one of the servants, and said, Behold, I have seen a son of Jesse the Bethlehemite, that is cunning in playing, and a mighty valiant man, and a man of war, and prudent in matters, and a comely person, and the LORD is with him. Wherefore Saul sent messengers unto Jesse, and said, Send me David thy son, which is with the sheep."

Please note that there are two types of gifts. They are:
1. People who are skilled at something.
2. People who are anointed to do something.

A skill is a learned craft. In short, the talent that the person has learned or become skilled at does not have any power backing it. There's nothing wrong with being skilled! We go to college to learn skills every day! But the anointing breaks yokes! This means that David was not only skilled at playing the lyre, he was an anointed minstrel, meaning whenever he worshiped God, a notable shift would take place in the spirit realm. This is what the anointing does. A natural action provokes a spiritual action or response. This also means that David's skills and abilities positioned him for the assignment that was on his life. That assignment was to rule over Israel. What about you?

Next, there are people who are anointed to accomplish certain feats. In other words, they are empowered by God to do something. The purpose of the anointing is to destroy yokes. Isaiah 10:27 reads, "And it shall come to pass in that day, that his burden shall be taken away from off thy shoulder, and his yoke from off thy neck, and the yoke shall be destroyed because of the anointing." Please understand that when this scripture says "his burden," it was referring to the Assyrians. Israel had been invaded by Syria during King Menahem's reign. In this, God was referring to the yoke or the burden that the Assyrians had placed upon the Hebrews by making them pay a yearly tribute to Assyria. But, what exactly is a yoke? Oxford Languages defines the word "yoke" as "a wooden crosspiece that is fastened over the necks of two animals and attached to the plow or cart that they are to pull." A yoke, in layman's terms, was a burden. It was a wooden piece placed on the necks or shoulders of two animals. This is because the tasks or assignments that the animals had been given were too burdensome for one animal, so a yoke would be placed on their necks. This would allow them to combine their strengths and share the burdens. As believers, we were, quite frankly, yoked to Satan through our sins. Our sins served as the wooden pieces that connected us with the kingdom of darkness. So, when God talks about destroying the yoke, He is talking about removing the crosspiece that connects us with the Mosaic Law and with sin. This would free us from Satan's control. After all, animals were typically equally yoked by farmers, but this wasn't always possible. It was not uncommon to see a smaller animal sharing a yoke with a bigger one. This allowed the bigger animal to grow stronger since it had to carry the majority of the burden, but it also burned out the smaller animal. This is similar to how Satan was dragging us around by our iniquities. So, when the Bible mentions someone being anointed, it means that they have the keys, the ability or the power to set the captives free in the name of Jesus. Please note that skilled people have gifts, but anointed people are gifts.

All the same, there are some people who are anointed to do a thing, but we always have to become skilled at whatever it is that we are anointed to do. For example, David was skilled at playing the lyre, but his anointing also got entangled in his skill-set. This allowed him to be both competent and potent when playing for the king. And just like David, most of us have skills. What are your skills? What are your unique abilities? What are you excellent at? Do you know what your purpose is? When asked about purpose, the average Christian immediately begins to think and talk about their jobs and whatever skills they are benefiting from financially. But your job isn't your purpose! Your job may be your calling or it may be tied to your calling. To get a better understanding, let's define the following words:

1. Identity
2. Purpose
3. Calling

Identity: The calling to your purpose; it is the cornerstone of your calling and your assignment. Ephesians 2:20-22 reads, "And are built upon the foundation of the apostles and prophets, Jesus Christ himself being the chief corner stone; in whom all the building fitly framed together groweth unto an holy temple in the Lord: In whom ye also are builded together for an habitation of God through the Spirit." A cornerstone was the first building block that they laid before laying the foundation of a building. As its name suggests, it was placed in the corner of the foundation; it is the rock in which the weight of the entire foundation rests. It was the largest stone, and it served as a guide to the builders, enabling them to lay the rest of the groundwork. Once the cornerstone had been put in place, the rest of the building would be made to conform to the angles and size of the cornerstone. For believers, our identities are what or who we identify with. We are made in the image of God, and our identity is singular; that is to be the expression of Christ in the Earth.

Purpose: We all have the same purpose, and that is to destroy the works of the devil. Think about the life of Moses. Moses had a purpose or, better yet, an assignment. His assignment was to deliver the Jews from Egypt and lead the Jews to the Promised Land. This is what he had been born for; this is what he had been abandoned for, and this is what he had been trained for! His gift would be fully activated in one moment, and that moment was the hour in which he'd stood in front of the Red Sea. Death surrounded him on every side, and the hopes and futures of the people rested on his shoulders at that moment. Moses was a deliverer. The same is true for Jesus. In short, our purpose is to be like Christ. Remember, we are made in the likeness of God. God is Spirit, so this isn't referencing our physical makeup; this scripture is speaking of our purpose or assignment. As believers, we all have the same assignment, which again is to be like Christ and to destroy the works or systems of Satan.

Calling: In Philippians 3:14, Apostle Paul went on record with these words, "I press toward the mark for the prize of the high calling of God in Christ Jesus." To understand what it means to be called, we have to look at instances in the scriptures when someone had been called or summoned. Let's look at the story of Samuel. 1 Samuel 3:2-9 reads, "And it came to pass at that time, when Eli was laid down in his place, and his eyes began to wax dim, that he could not see; and ere the lamp of God went out in the temple of the LORD, where the ark of God was, and Samuel was laid down to sleep; that the LORD called Samuel: and he answered, Here am I. And he ran unto Eli, and said, Here am I; for thou calledst me. And he said, I called not; lie down again. And he went and lay down. And the LORD called yet again, Samuel. And Samuel arose and went to Eli, and said, Here am I; for thou didst call me. And he answered, I called not, my son; lie down again. Now Samuel did not yet know the LORD, neither was the word of the LORD yet revealed unto him. And the LORD called Samuel again the third time. And he arose and went to Eli, and said,

Here am I; for thou didst call me. And Eli perceived that the LORD had called the child. Therefore Eli said unto Samuel, Go, lie down: and it shall be, if he call thee, that thou shalt say, Speak, LORD; for thy servant heareth. So Samuel went and lay down in his place." In this, we find the young Samuel in the infancy of his gifting. He was wired to be a prophet, but according to the scriptures, at this time, he did not know the Lord. Consequently, the moment the Lord called him, he didn't know God's voice, so he assumed that his mentor had called him. It wasn't until the Lord called Samuel a total of three times before Eli realized that the young boy's ears had been opened, meaning it was time for him to be trained in the prophetic so that he could begin to fulfill his purpose on the Earth. Samuel was a prophet of God; this was his identity, and he had the same calling that you have and the same calling that I have; that is to destroy the works of the enemy. But how he would do this is what we refer to as a calling. Samuel had been identified as a prophet, but his calling was to serve as a prophet to King Saul and to King David. This is the position of his purpose.

You may be an evangelist, but what are your means of evangelism? This is your calling. For example, there are some men and women who are called to evangelize in the roughest neighborhoods. Many of them were raised in bad neighborhoods and in deplorable conditions. Some of them have even served time in prison or once lived a life that is frowned upon by society. But when God saved them, He didn't call them to Beverly Hills. He assigned them to a specific demographic, and while they may not look like you and I, they are incredibly effective when they are in the midst of the people they're called to. This is when their anointings come alive! This is where their confidence stands tall! They are not afraid to go into the most dangerous neighborhoods and approach people who society has given up on. They put their lives in danger everyday to win souls. And if you speak with them, you will discover that fear doesn't have a grip on them. They love what they do and who they are, because they've come to love the Lord!

In short, your purpose is to destroy the works of the enemy, and your calling is the means by which you will destroy the enemy's works. We accomplish these through our gifts. And please note that your calling doesn't have to be associated with a religious title. You may be called to work in a nursing home, and it is there that your grace is awakened. In the nursing home, your assignment is to introduce the residents to Christ, and not only that, but to help them to tap into the benefits of the Kingdom. Additionally, your calling may be to ensure that their wisdom doesn't go to waste. You may be a conduit of wisdom or a teacher, but before you can teach, you have to acquire the knowledge that you'll need for the audience that you're called to. You may be called to work in the music industry, and not necessarily on the gospel side of that industry. In this, your assignment may not be to make music that wins souls, but to convert the hearts of the people who make music. God looks at the bigger picture because He is the bigger picture! What I mean by this is, traditionally speaking, the church has been ineffective at winning souls because we were trying to stay within our own (very) limited corners, making music for other Christians and shunning everyone who created non-Christian music. Meaning, we have not always been great at evangelism. But God knows that if He can win the heart of, for example, Megan the Stallion, He could also reach her audience. So, God does send spies into this industry to go after people like Megan. He's not only concerned with their listeners' souls, but He loves them as well. Hear me—if He'll send Daniel into a Babylonian castle to serve a pagan king named Nebuchadnezzar, and use Daniel to convert the heart of the king, He'll send men and women into Hollywood to win the hearts of some of today's most perverted and rebellious celebrities.

There are levels of giftings; this is why there are low-level gifts, just as there are high-level gifts. The thing is, every level of gifting is needed, but the problem is that many creative gifts don't respect the levels, systems or industries they are called to. Because of this, they forsake their assignments in favor of doing whatever it is that they want to do. In the world of ministry, we call this "being off post." This reminds me of what Jesus' disciples did in one of His darkest hours. They fell asleep! They could not watch for the enemy because they were counting sheep! Also, consider the parable of the tares. Matthew 13:24-28 reads, "Another parable put he forth unto them, saying, The kingdom of heaven is likened unto a man which sowed good seed in his field: But while men slept, his enemy came and sowed tares among the wheat, and went his way. But when the blade was sprung up, and brought forth fruit, then appeared the tares also. So the servants of the householder came and said unto him, Sir, didst not thou sow good seed in thy field? From whence then hath it tares? He said unto them, An enemy hath done this." When we are not on post, the enemy creeps in; this is why we have to respect the levels and systems that we are called to. All the same, we have to respect the laws of those levels and systems.

Again, there are levels of giftings. This means that in the world of hairdressers, there is rank. In the world of science, there is rank. In the world of art, there is rank. In the world of medicine, there is rank. Think about surgeons. Not all surgeons earn the same amount of money or have the same amount of respect in their industry. This is because some surgeons are far more knowledgeable and understanding about the human body than their colleagues. In order for them to become as competent as they are, they had to do the one thing that most creatives seem to be allergic to. They had to make several sacrifices. These sacrifices included, but are not limited to:

1. Staying up later to study.
2. Arriving at their jobs earlier than their co-workers.
3. Staying later at their jobs.
4. Investing in more study materials.
5. Taking time out of their schedules to glean from men and women who outrank them.

6. Relocating. Some people have to move to other states or countries to attend better schools or to intern under the people they want to glean from.
7. Travel to seminars, conferences and gatherings so that they could acquire more information.

This means that there were seasons when these surgeons were likely making less money than their counterparts who'd gone immediately into working. In every world, you have to be futuristic in your thinking because people who are impatient almost always end up settling and becoming low-ranking gifts in the industries they are called to. And again, being a low-ranking gift isn't necessarily bad, after all, every world has dimensions, and we need creatives on every one of these levels, but if you want to ascend in any given world, you have to be willing to make the necessary sacrifices, and you will have to make more sacrifices than most of the people there. Let's take a closer look at the word "sacrifice."

The word "sacrifice" (verb), according to Oxford Languages, is defined as "offer or kill as a religious sacrifice." In reality, a sacrifice is an offering. It is the act of exchanging one thing for another. And it's not a sacrifice unless it hurts. Some of today's biggest celebrities have rags to riches stories where they had to make some pretty pronounced sacrifices in order to finance their dreams. And it was those sacrifices that caused them to stand out from their peers because it revealed their hunger and allowed them to grow in competence. Consider the sacrifices that Abraham had to make to become the father of faith.

1. He had to leave his friends, family and comforts behind.
2. He had to follow God, not knowing where he was being led to. In other words, he had to walk by faith and not by sight.
3. He had to wait until he was 100-years old before he would have his first (legitimate) son.
4. He had to send his firstborn (illegitimate) son away at his wife's request.

These are just a few sacrifices that he had to make to accomplish his assignment. This brings to mind Newton's First Law of Motion, which says that "an object at rest remains at rest, and an object in motion remains in motion at a constant speed and in a straight line unless acted on by an unbalanced force." What this means is, you will get out of life whatever it is that you put in it. Billy Preston simplified it with, "Nothing from nothing leaves nothing." Proverbs 13:4 says it this way, "The soul of the sluggard desireth, and hath nothing: but the soul of the diligent shall be made fat." 2 Corinthians 9:6 also reminds us, "But this I say, He which soweth sparingly shall reap also sparingly; and he which soweth bountifully shall reap also bountifully." In short, if you want to increase in competence, you have to be willing to make a small or great sacrifice, but the size or level of your competence will never outgrow the size or level of your sacrifice. This is pure thermodynamics at work. The following information was taken from How Stuff Works:

"Thermodynamics is the study of how energy works in a system, whether it's an engine or Earth's core. It can be reduced to several basic laws, which Snow cleverly summed up as follows [source: Physics Planet]:

- You can't win.
- You can't break even.
- You can't quit the game.

Let's unpack these a bit. By saying you can't win, Snow meant that since matter and energy are conserved, you can't get one without giving up some of the other (i.e., $E=mc^2$). It also means that for an engine to produce work, you have to supply heat, although in anything other than a perfectly closed system, some heat is inevitably lost to the outside world, which then leads to the second law.

The second statement — you can't break even — means that due to ever-increasing entropy, you can't return to the same energy state. Energy concentrated in one place will always flow to places of lower concentration.

Finally, the third law — you can't quit the game — refers to absolute zero, the lowest theoretical temperature possible, measured at zero Kelvin or (minus 273.15 degrees Celsius and minus 459.67 degrees Fahrenheit). When a system reaches absolute zero, molecules stop all movement, meaning that there is no kinetic energy, and entropy reaches its lowest possible value. But in the real world, even in the recesses of space, reaching absolutely zero is impossible — you can only get very close to it" (Source: How Stuff Works/10 Scientific Laws You Really Should Know/Jacob Silverman).

In every system, sacrifice is needed. As believers, our sacrifices usually consist of us giving up the things that we want the most and leaving our places of comfort in order to accomplish our assignments. Tyler Perry wouldn't be where he is today if he hadn't saved money for his plays by sleeping in his car. And of course, there's no telling where we would be today if it weren't for the sacrifices made by Martin Luther King, Jr., Sojourner Truth, W.E.B. Du Bois, Rosa Parks and the list goes on. The point is, great men and women do what's hard in order to make a change in this Earth and in order to eradicate demonic systems, all the while helping to birth out Kingdom systems. Remember, we are vessels, and just like blood vessels, we have to stay connected to the True Vine; this way, His will can and will be done in the Earth. Needless to say, staying within the confines of God's will is no easy task because there are distractions and temptations that compete for our attention every single day. But the third law of thermodynamics dictates that we simply cannot quit, no matter what we experience, what we want or how we feel. Instead, we must continue to grow in stature (anointing, maturity and competence) until we reach our high-calling in Christ Jesus and we execute what we were designed to accomplish. This is how we grow in competence; this is how we capture the attention of kings and queens!

"The important thing is this: to be ready at any moment to sacrifice what you are for what you could become."
~Charles Dickens

"If you want something you've never had, you must be willing to do something you've never done."
~Anonymous

The Timeline of a Gift

The word "Chronos" means time. According to Oxford Languages, the word "chronology" is defined as "the arrangement of events or dates in the order of their occurrence." They both come from the prefix "chrono," which means "relating to time" (Oxford Languages). Again, time is an ordered event. The best way to explain this is through the law of sowing and reaping. Galatians 6:7 details this law; it reads, "Be not deceived; God is not mocked: for whatsoever a man soweth, that shall he also reap." But what is sowing, and what exactly is reaping? The following definitions were taken from Oxford Languages.

- **Sow:** plant (seed) by scattering it on or in the earth.
- **Reap:** cut or gather (a crop or harvest); receive (a reward or benefit) as a consequence of one's own or other people's actions.

God uses the concept of a garden to describe this principle and law. This is because our lives are a perpetual state of sowing and then reaping. These are what we call choices and consequences, and of course, consequences can be good or they can be bad. Either way, whatever you put in this world, you can expect to reap it. And unfortunately, we reap from the choices of others as well, namely, our parents. This is because some seeds can take years to grow, and they aren't around to reap when those seeds reach full maturity. This is what we call a generational curse. Think of a tree. Coco De Mer Trees can take between 20-40 years to reach full maturity, cherry trees can take between 4-7 years and pear trees can take between 4-6 years. But there are some trees that reach full maturity within a year or two. And then again, there are some ordered events that we will find ourselves in. For example, we know that New Years' Eve will take place every year on December 31st, just as January 1st is New Year's Day. Then again, there are some events that are not necessarily annual, but they are scheduled to take place. The point is, there are somethings coming your way that are the result of your choices, your parents' choices or the choices of the people closest to you. Then again, there are some events that will occur in your life because God has scheduled you to go through them. All of these events are designed to push you in one direction or the other. On the spectrum of good and evil, there are only two directions, and they are right and wrong. Howbeit, every event that we find ourselves in and everything that we reap has wisdom in it, if we would only pray about it. A man slams his motorcycle into a tree, and while this is horrible, there's wisdom in that moment. Wisdom would tell him to slow down, wear his helmet and pay attention, and while this may appear to be low-level wisdom, it is wisdom nonetheless, and wisdom on all levels can save your life.

Every creative gift has a timeline, and by creative, I don't necessarily mean that you're a painter, a dancer or an actor. You may be a mechanic. Creativity isn't always colorful or visually appealing! A mechanic's job is to make sure that every part of a car is working and in order, but more than that, mechanics have to be creative and innovative all the time. They sometimes repair parts and systems in unorthodox ways that actually work in order to save their customers money. Herding sheep isn't a pretty job, but shepherds have to be creative because all of their sheep have personalities, strengths, weaknesses and they are all at certain stages of maturity. Some sheep are always trying to escape, while there are others that simply refuse to eat. And then, there are those sheep that are combative. A shepherd has to innovate and find ways to fix all of these problems and to prevent them from occurring in the future.

Again, every creative gift has a timeline. This means that there are somethings that we all must go through to get to something in particular. Think of seasons. There's no way around it. You have to go through Winter to get to Fall. This is especially true if you remain in the same geographical location. All the same, if you're driving from one state to another, there are certain cities and states that you have to go through. You may be able to go around some of these cities by going through other cities, but you have to endure the process of traveling, and there are certain places and experiences that you will have to go through if you want to arrive at a specific place at a specific time. The same is true in life. If you want to become a doctor, you have to go to college and you have to go to medical school. You also have to take certain classes in accordance with the area of medicine you want to specialize in. You can't just go to college and take whatever classes you want and expect to someday become a doctor. For example, maybe you want to become a graphic designer. Now, some people could argue that the world of graphic design is overpopulated, but this isn't true. There are no fields that are truly over-saturated or overpopulated. The real problem is, the bottom of every field is always packed. These are the mountains that most folks aren't willing to climb. Consequently, we have a bunch of low-level gifts competing for business, and this drives down the value of whatever it is that they are selling. This is what we call a buyers' market. Oxford Languages defines the phrase "buyer's market" this way, "an economic situation in which goods or shares are plentiful and buyers can keep prices down." Howbeit, there are graphic designers out there who are making more money than some of these doctors! This is because they made more sacrifices than their counterparts to get where they are today! What this means for you is that, even though there is a timeline and a spectrum to your emergence, it is possible for you to forfeit the height of your calling in order to remain comfortable. Apostle Paul said, "I press toward the mark for the prize of the high calling of God in Christ Jesus" (Philippians 3:). What are you pressing towards? Let's look at the life of one of the most decorated and renowned gifts to ever enter this Earth: Harriet Tubman.

Known as the Black Moses, Harriet Tubman would help to lead over 300 slaves to freedom. Howbeit, her emergence hadn't been an easy one. The following timeline was taken from Biography.com.

Month/Year	Event
c. 1828	Tubman is about five or six years old when her enslavers hire her out to tend to an infant. She is whipped for any perceived mistakes.
c. 1829	Around the age of seven, Tubman is again hired out. Her duties include walking into wet marshes to check muskrat traps. She becomes ill with measles and returns to her mother to recover.
c. 1834-36	An overseer throws a two-pound weight at another slave but hits Tubman's head. She barely survives the devastating injury and experiences headaches for the remainder of her life. It's possible this injury led to her suffering from temporal lobe epilepsy, which could explain her visions and sleeping spells.
c. 1835	Tubman works as a field hand, which she prefers to inside tasks.
c. 1830s	Two of Tubman's older sisters are sold and transported out of Maryland.
1840	Tubman's father is freed from slavery.

1844	She weds John Tubman, a free Black man, though her status as a slave means the union is not legally recognized. Upon marriage, Tubman adopts her mother's name of Harriet.
03/07/49	Tubman's owner dies, which makes her fear being sold.
09/17/49	Tubman heads north with two of her brothers to escape slavery. However, the men become nervous and convince their sister to return.
10/49	Tubman runs away. She follows the North Star and makes it to Philadelphia. As Pennsylvania is a free state, she has escaped enslavement.
09/18/50	The Fugitive Slave Act of 1850 passes. It requires all parts of the United States, even states that had outlawed slavery, to participate in the return of runaway slaves.
December 1850	Tubman helps rescue a niece and her niece's children after learning they are supposed to be sold at auction.
1851	Tubman tries to bring her husband north, but he decides to remain with his second wife, a free Black woman. Tubman instead guides another group

	to Canada, where they will be outside the reach of the Fugitive Slave Act.
December 1854	Tubman helps a group that includes three of her brothers travel to Canada.
June 1857	Tubman brings her parents from Maryland to Canada. Her father is in danger because he has been helping the Underground Railroad.
April 1858	In Canada, Tubman meets abolitionist John Brown. She learns of his plans to spark a slave rebellion in the United States and agrees to gather recruits for the cause.
1859	Tubman purchases a property in Auburn, New York, from antislavery politician William H. Seward. Having been unhappy in Canada, her parents join Tubman there.
04/27/60	In Troy, New York, Tubman helps former slave Charles Nalle elude the U.S. marshals who intend to return him to his enslaver.
12/01/60	Tubman makes her last trip on the Underground Railroad

(Source: Biography.com/Harriet Tubman: Timeline of Her Life, Underground Rail Service and Activism/Sara Kettler)

Please note that this is not the completed timeline of Harriet's life and activism. She would go on to serve as a spy for the Union army. Additionally, she would help to free more than 700 slaves in South Carolina when she'd led an armed raid up the Combahee River, and the list of her accomplishments goes on. But hear me—it all started with a whipping and it progressed from there. Harriet just knew that she couldn't spend the entirety of her life being beat, spat on and mistreated simply because of the color of her skin. This is how gifts emerge. They often experience one or more incidents that almost feel unbearable to them. They look around and notice that everyone else seems complacent. When you are a high-level gift, you begin to ask yourself the following questions:

- Why am I not settled? Everyone else seems to be okay with the situation.
- Am I crazy? Is there something wrong with me?
- Why can't others see what I see or feel what I feel?!
- Who am I to question what no one else seems to be questioning?

When you are gifted, these questions become more than just thoughts, they become burdens. This is the emerging or promotion of a gift. It's when the creative begins to show signs of maturity. These signs include, but are not limited to:

1. The gift begins to volunteer. Rather than complaining, the individual puts his or her hands to the plow.
2. The gift becomes more solution-minded than problem-centered.

3. The gift becomes a gift, instead of a burden, meaning the individual begins to give more than he or she takes from any given system or organization.
4. The gift helps himself or herself, and then begins to help others. This is the proverbial "removing of the speck from one's own eye, so that we can see clearly enough to remove it from our neighbors' eyes."
5. The gift lays down his or her life for his or her assignment. This is called sacrifice, and by life, I mean personal desires.

There may have been a moment or a season where Harriet considered returning to slavery so that she could be with her husband, but her gift was far too great by then to be contained in such a limited space. (Note: once a gift comes out of its container, it is nearly impossible to get it back in.) So, she made a major sacrifice to fulfill her assignment. And as she began to emerge, wanted posters began to surface around town with her face on them. She now had a bounty on her head. Hear me—you have not stepped into your purpose until you capture the attention and the interest of high-ranking demonic authorities! You haven't made your mark in the Earth until demons that aren't even assigned to you know your name!

Acts 19:13-20: Then certain of the vagabond Jews, exorcists, took upon them to call over them which had evil spirits the name of the Lord Jesus, saying, We adjure you by Jesus whom Paul preacheth. And there were seven sons of one Sceva, a Jew, and chief of the priests, which did so. And the evil spirit answered and said, Jesus I know, and Paul I know; but who are ye? And the man in whom the evil spirit was leaped on them, and overcame them, and prevailed against them, so that they fled out of that house naked and wounded. And this was known to all the Jews and Greeks also dwelling at Ephesus; and fear fell on them all, and the name of the Lord Jesus was magnified. And many that believed came, and confessed, and shewed their deeds. Many of them also which used curious arts brought their books together, and burned them before all men: and they counted the price of them, and found it fifty thousand pieces of silver. So mightily grew the word of God and prevailed.

The sons of Sceva hadn't undergone the process; they didn't know Jesus! This is why they said to the demon, "We adjure you by Jesus who Paul preaches about." This only enraged that devil! It wasn't assigned to Paul, but it knew his name! Do you know how many Christians are out there who are complete strangers to the hosts of hell? Sure, many of them are demon-bound, but most demons don't know their names because they haven't stepped outside of themselves to even become a remote threat, even to the demons that they are wrestling with! And if hell doesn't know us, how do we expect the Most High God to know us? Because obviously, we haven't been in His face like we should have!

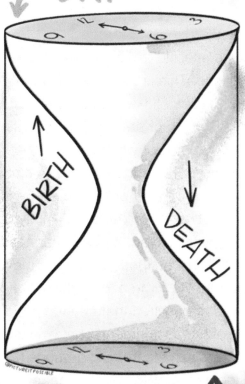

Matthew 7:21-23: Not every one that saith unto me, Lord, Lord, shall enter into the kingdom of heaven; but he that doeth the will of my Father which is in heaven. Many will say to me in that day, Lord, Lord, have we not prophesied in thy name? And in thy name have cast out devils? And in thy name done many wonderful works? And then will I profess unto them, I never knew you: depart from me, ye that work iniquity.

We have to be in the will of God in order to attract the attention of God! We have to seek Him to find Him! All the same, there are specific events that must take place before a gift's emergence. This is the timeline of that particular creative. Earlier on, we talked about order. The space between the beginning or dawning of your assignment versus the peak, climax or what some call your "grand finale" is called a process. This is the wilderness that every gift must enter and overcome. For example, Harriet's wilderness was the space between Maryland to Pennsylvania, which was a total of 90 miles. Now, this was her natural wilderness, but the real wilderness experience began the moment she decided to risk her life for freedom, all the way up to the moment when she obtained that freedom. And that was just the beginning of her assignment! That was the starting line of her race! It was just the training grounds for her purpose. Her real assignment or wilderness experience would be initiated the moment she looked outside of herself and decided to go back and help other slaves to obtain their freedom. This is the making or the emergence of a leader.

Leading herself through the underground railroad had been an arduous enough task, but the real challenge would be leading bound people to freedom, many of whom had grown comfortable with their chains. Understand that a bound person would much rather help to bind others than he would to endure the process needed to get him to freedom. This is why pastoring is such a messy and dangerous job. Pastors have to lead people who don't necessarily want to be led or free. We have to clean them up, inform them, correct them and let them throw their tantrums. We then have to move forward while they are in the middle of those tantrums. Hear me—I know that we like to think of the people who Harriet led as sweet, loving and humble people, but the truth is, Harriet had to lead a bunch of stiff-necked, traumatized, fearful and uneducated people towards a freedom that they had never experienced, and believe me, this was harder than she gets credited for! When leading broken and bound people, you have to be ready, willing and strong enough to carry a lot of dead weight. This doesn't mean that you will have to drag anyone to freedom, after all, you cannot legally infringe upon the will of another human. But it does mean that you will deal with a lot of opposition from the very people you are trying to help. This is what the military refers to as friendly fire, and according to the statistics, friendly fire is responsible for up to 20 percent of the deaths that occur in battle. This is because fear will turn your friends into your enemies in an instance, especially high-level fear. Consider this story. The curtains have been open for five minutes, and the only thing that could be heard was a few coughs coming from the audience. The dark stage begins to suddenly illuminate, and out of the shadows, the crowd can see a form emerging. She is dressed in a black tutu and a black shirt to match. The dancer lifts one of her feet, bending her knee and pointing her right foot towards her left knee. Her left leg is slightly bent as well, and she's standing on the tips of her toes. The music begins to play as if it is creeping up on the audience, and that's when the once still figure begins to move. She sways to the left, and then to the right, before turning so eloquently, showing off her agility.

At the front of the crowd sits an unpaid critic. His name is Sherman, and even though he is unemployed, Sherman is a depressed and miserable critic who's living off his inheritance. The dancer's job is to entertain, to inspire and to communicate to the people in the audience through the art of dance. This is an opportunity for Sherman to be inspired and to feel a measure of joy. This is his opportunity to escape depression, if but for a brief moment. What Sherman does with this moment will determine how his day goes or maybe even his week. But Sherman is a critic, meaning he's critical of everything. The dancer is trying to help him and others, but Sherman refuses to be helped. This is because Sherman wrestles with or, better yet, is submitted to a strongman named Entitlement. He sees life and people through a very narrow lens. So, while the dancer has the ability to lead him to the doorway of freedom, Sherman has to be willing to be led. Then again, there are more sinister examples than this. A sergeant in the military could be leading his men through a forest and away from the front-lines of a battle. The fighting has grown intense, and they've already lost a few soldiers, but the sergeant is determined to not lose another man or woman to the opposition. So, he leads them through the darkness, into swamps and through a series of caves. This is what the wilderness looks like. This is what it looks like to put your gift on display. But he cannot lead anyone who doesn't want to be led. He cannot put his entire squadron at risk just because one of his soldiers is complaining about being tired. Sure, in the military, they promote the adage, "No man left behind," but this doesn't always look like someone who isn't injured being carried. It may look like him being dragged or threatened, and one of the reasons they won't leave someone like this behind is because he is proving himself to be weak. This means that if the opposing army was to find him, he'd happily tell them everything that they wanted to know, thus, putting his entire squadron or the military's mission at risk. What I'm attempting to prove here is this— the highest and most pronounced part of our assignments take place when we emerge as leaders because this is the time when we have to regurgitate what we've learned through our own personal journeys. This is the time when we deal with the most warfare and the most friendly fire. And the hardest part of it all is trying to lead victims to victory. Believe it or not, most victims like being seen as victims because they adore the attention that comes with it. Imagine trying to lead someone out of bondage who likes being bound. Then again, there are those creative gifts who will want to quit simply because they don't want to stand out.

"Can I give it back? What happens if I just try to lead a normal life?" The tears begin to stream down her face as she allows these words to escape her lips. "I'm tired," she says. "I'm just so tired." Sitting across from her is not easy. As a matter of fact, I've sat opposite of many creative gifts who've asked me these questions. When they'd received the many prophetic words about the industries they had been called to and the many accomplishments they were set to make in those industries, they'd received those words with glee. But the moment that persecution arose because of that word, they were ready to fall away or, better yet, give up. Normal, to the creative, is the equivalent of death. It is not normal for a creative to be normal! So, I've had to be the bearer of what they considered to be bad news. Outside of their purpose, they would never find peace. They weren't created to flourish in normality. Their chemical makeup wouldn't allow it. They needed to press through the pressures and the persecutions to get to the other side of the seasons they were in. They were in the wilderness season, and they'd just started getting their first whiffs of what it means to grow weary. The journey just felt unbearable, but the wilderness is necessary! It helps to prune them of everything that is Egyptian, and it is designed to cultivate their character. There are certain characteristics, strengths and levels of maturity that they have to have when they step into their destinies, otherwise, their assignments will swallow them whole. And the wilderness is a space carved out for the creative to be cultivated in. This is the period of grace. This is the time when the creative deals with his greatest warfare because the smell of Egypt, the habits or strongholds formed in Egypt and the diet of the Egyptian all have a grip on the gift's potential. While the gift may have physically escaped Egypt, Pharaoh still has a hold on the gift's heart and the law of works still has a grip on the gift's potential. Nevertheless, this is all marked on the gift's timeline. But the gift will continue to go in circles if there is no one there to lead him or her. This is why every creative needs a pastor. Again, there are some events that the gift will endure because of his or her choices, the choices of his or her parents and/or ancestors, and the choices of the people closest to the individual. Then again, there are some events that are scheduled to take place on a specific date at a specific time. And hear me—the creative can (and oftentimes does) sabotage these events when they are not ready! The goal is to mature the gift, and maturity doesn't take place in a vacuum; it's not an automatic event that takes place by happenstance. It has to be cultivated through a specific diet of information and experiences. Even though she didn't want it, Harriet needed her husband to release her so that she could become the legend that she is today. She couldn't be normal, after all, normality for a slave was far from pleasant. Then again, there were slaves who had grown used to the abuse and were comfortable with the dysfunction. Yes, there were slaves who had Stockholm's Syndrome! What is Stockholm's Syndrome?

"Stockholm syndrome is a psychological response. It occurs when hostages or abuse victims bond with their captors or abusers. This psychological connection develops over the course of the days,

147

weeks, months, or even years of captivity or abuse. With this syndrome, hostages or abuse victims may come to sympathize with their captors. This is the opposite of the fear, terror, and disdain that might be expected from the victims in these situations. Over the course of time, some victims do come to develop positive feelings toward their captors. They may even begin to feel as if they share common goals and causes. The victim may begin to develop negative feelings toward the police or authorities. They may resent anyone who may be trying to help them escape from the dangerous situation they're in. This paradox does not happen with every hostage or victim, and it's unclear why it occurs when it does. Many psychologists and medical professionals consider Stockholm syndrome a coping mechanism, or a way to help victims handle the trauma of a terrifying situation. Indeed, the history of the syndrome may help explain why that is" (Source: Healthline.com/What is Stockholm's Syndrome and Who Does it Affect?)

What about you? What has your timeline looked like, and have you grown comfortable with chaos? Every creative gift must question and challenge himself or herself! Every creative gift must correct and stretch himself or herself! You will never be normal. The first order of business is to make peace with this and then say "yes" to the call that's on your life. You are in time, even though you may not necessarily be on time, but God can accelerate your promotion if you would simply get in His will and allow Him to process you! Start sowing the right seeds so that you can reap the right harvest! And lastly, don't allow "normal" people to make you feel bad about being a gift!

• LEADERSHIP •

The Era of Gifts

Below, you'll find a short list of some Old Testament biblical gifts and the eras they reigned.

Name and Era	Major Accomplishment
Abraham c. 1996 BC-1821 BC	Became the father of the faith by following God and embarking on a long faith-walk. Today, there are three Abrahamic religions: Christianity, Judaism and Islam.
Moses 1400 BC	Confronted Pharaoh and helped the Hebrews to escape from Egypt. He also led them towards the Promised Land.
Joseph 1600 to 1700 BC	Joseph is known for his faith-based resilience and his integrity. His story details one of both chaos and conquest.
Ruth 1100 BC	She chose to forsake the pagan god of her family and follow after YAHWEH. This was demonstrated through her choice to continue on with her mother-in-law, Naomi, after her husband's death.
David 1000 BCE	The writer of Psalms and referred to by God as a man after His own heart, David demonstrated faith, honor and perseverance in the face of adversity.
Esther 492 BC.–c. 460 BC	Helped to save the Jews from the wrath of Haman through her faith, humility and boldness.
John, the Baptist 1 BC	Set the stage for the arrival of Jesus Christ, and he also baptized Jesus.
Jesus Christ 1 BC	The Messiah; the Savior of the World! Ushered in the New Testament and gave His life so that mankind could be reconciled to God.

The Creative's Diet

There are 12 dishes that the emerging gift must eat before he or she arrives in purpose on purpose, but before we dive into this lesson, let's break down time as we know it:

- There are 12 months in a year.
- There are 365 days in a year.
- There are 8,760 hours in a year.
- There are 31 days in most months.
- There are 4 weeks in a month.
- There are 7 days in a week.
- There are 24 hours in a single day.
- There are 60 minutes in every hour.
- There are 60 seconds in every minute.
- There are 1,000 milliseconds in a second.

And then, there are nanoseconds and microseconds, but we won't get into that. We'll look at the standard clock in several ways. First and foremost, there are 12 numbers on a clock, all of which represent an hour. Imagine these all being slices of a single pie. Everyone has their own slice of the pie, and it goes without saying that some people simply don't like pie, so when their hour comes, they won't do any work. They'll just sell their pie for comfort, much like Esau did with his birthright. In layman's terms, most gifts reject their assignments. Some people keep putting it off, not realizing that they are essentially rejecting themselves and their assignments because you can't tell time to stop when your hour comes. David had to fight Goliath in the hour that he did because he didn't have the ability to push that war back until he felt strong enough, anointed enough or old enough to fight the giant. When the moment presented itself, he had to make a decision. Either he was going to step into his destiny and do what he had been designed to do, or he would let someone else fight Goliath. David felt something waking up in him in that hour that he could not explain. "Who is this uncircumcised Philistine that should defy the army of the living God?!" David's frustration wasn't anger, it was righteous indignation. This is the moment when the heart of God merges with the heart of a man, and the man can feel what God feels. David was in this moment, and thankfully, he had been prepared for it.

The Hand You're Dealt

There are three hands on a standard analog clock. They are the hour hand, the minute hand and the second hand. The second hand is in constant movement, the minute hand moves every 60 seconds, and the hour hand moves every 60 minutes. This means that they don't all move at the same rate; they all have a function and an assignment, and while we may not use analog clocks as much these days as we used to use them in times past, they are still effective at helping us tell time. Let's imagine that some of us were hour hands, some of us were minute hands and some of us were second hands, and the clocks that we are fastened to represent the worlds that we are called to. Imagine that you were an hour hand. You can't move until the minute hand has made its rounds, and the minute hand can't move until the second hand has made its rounds. It would even appear that they move faster than you and more than you, but this race isn't given to the swift; patience wins the game. And remember, we talked about target audiences. In short, you are not called to everyone, so as you make your rounds around that clock, there are certain hours when your audience will be asleep, meaning no one will support you, no one will celebrate you and no one will notice you. But you'll hear others around you being celebrated as they make their rounds, some more than others. You may be tempted at any given time to quit and you may be tempted to stall, but if you don't move as often as you should be moving, the world that you're called to may consider you broken or ineffective. In other words, you'll end up with a bad reputation. This is the hand you've been dealt, and how you play it will determine what your next season looks like. You see, in every given season, you are given a set of seeds. Your job isn't just to plant those seeds, your job is to plant those seeds in the right places and position yourself around people who will water those seeds. And there are different types of seeds in your hand; there are seeds from your past, seeds from your present and seeds from your future. Let's look at the seeds from your past. With these seeds, you have to be careful because they don't need too much sunlight, and you can't let them root themselves in the unconscious level of your mind; this is the place where trauma is stored, and while these are the seeds of traumatic events, you can't store them as trauma. They are testimonies. These are the seeds that you are to feed those who come behind you. You can't eat these seeds or water these seeds. You have to package them up and market them to others.

Next, there are seeds from your present. You have to be careful that you don't mix these up with the seeds from your past, because when these two overlap, unforgiveness is inevitable. Additionally, you have to be careful that you don't eat these seeds. These seeds contain the testimonies of others, what you've learned from past experiences, the information that you've studied, what you've been taught and what you've come to believe. As you make your rounds around your personalized clock, you have to carefully drop these seeds in the right places. For example, the hour will come when you'll meet your Goliath. In this hour, you can't testify to your Goliath; he doesn't care about who you are or what you've been through. You can't throw your degree at your Goliath; there's a space and a time for that. In this particular hour, you have to draw from your past experiences. You have to remember what you've learned when you were fighting with the bears and the lions! In this hour, you have to also take up the Word that is (or should be) stored in your heart. David reached into his bag and grabbed one of the five stones he'd gathered; this represented the Chief Cornerstone, the Rock that the builders had rejected, and he used the Rock to slay Goliath.

And finally, there are the seeds for your future. These are the dreams and the plans that you have. At some point, you will find that you may have to use these seeds to fend off or distract the birds of prey. You've held onto them for many years, thinking that certain events were going to come to pass, and it can be quite the challenge the moment that you realize that God is requiring you to give them up. What this means is, you have to sacrifice your plans for you in favor of God's plans for you. All the same, there are doors that you may have access to, and while God has given you access to these doors, He hasn't given you the keys to open them. Hear me—you will see windows of opportunity that will allow you to access what was meant for your future. But remember John 10:1, where Jesus says, "Verily, verily, I say unto you, He that entereth not by the door into the sheepfold, but climbeth up some other way, the same is a thief and a robber." This means that there are legal ways to enter into a season, just as there are illegal ways to enter into a season. A perfect example of this is a woman who wants to be married by a certain time. She meets and begins to date a man who God, Himself has sent into her life. But there's a "not yet" surrounding them getting serious about one another. This is because, in that particular season, the man of her dreams is not necessarily the man of God's dreams, meaning he isn't fully ready to be a husband just yet. He's saved, sanctified, filled with the Holy Spirit, but at the same time, he's still slightly double-minded. God knows that he is on the verge of his breakthrough; he's been studying His Bible, getting therapy and going through deliverance, but he can't be too distracted in this hour. It is for this reason that God says to the young woman, "Back off." In other words,

God wants the man's full attention. Then again, God wants to test her heart as well. Will she prioritize God's command over her own desires, or she will fall into the trap of idolatry? She chooses the ladder, so the perversion that God wanted to deal with in the man's heart has somewhere to express itself. One day, she receives a call from her boyfriend and he claims to have a flat tire. "Can you come to the Starbucks on 5th and Lawson? I left my jack in the trunk of your car." She agrees. And after he repairs his tire, he asks his girlfriend to trail him to his house. Let's call them Vivian and Henry.

Once they pull into Henry's driveway, he exits his car and makes his way over to Vivian's car. He then gets into the passenger's seat and the two begin to talk. Up until that point, they've been keeping everything holy, and they have no plans to do anything off-putting that night, but the mood immediately shifts mid-conversation. Henry looks at Vivian, and he has an authentic moment. "You know, since the moment I met you, I knew I'd marry you. Viv, I love you with everything in me. I remember that time we went to that conference in Texas. Every prophet that came over to us kept talking about how God had brought us together and how He was going to use us as a power couple. Can I be honest? I held it together, but I wanted to cry. You are more than my dream girl, you are my everything. And I can't wait to marry you, make babies you with and just wake up next to you." These words prick Vivian's unguarded heart. Henry has always been loving and he's always said the right things, but something about this moment feels different. For whatever reason, she feels the need to reciprocate, but she doesn't have the words to do this moment justice, so she leans in close to her boyfriend and the two begin to kiss. The kissing grows intense, and the two find themselves nearly putting the car into drive. That's when Henry suddenly stops and says, "Man, I don't know how much longer I can wait. Baby, I need you. Do you hear me? I need you. *(Sighs)*. Let me go in the house before we end up doing something we shouldn't be doing." These words seem noble enough, and just as Henry exits the vehicle, Vivian realizes that she's not ready to end their night together. The moment feels so magical, and Vivian feels almost drunk. "See you later, babe," Henry says as he slowly makes his way away from her vehicle, but neither of them is ready to end that moment. "Hold up," Vivian says shouting out her window. "Want some company?" And we all know how this story ends. Vivian didn't realize it at the moment, but she was being seduced because her boyfriend wasn't done processing. And because she wouldn't distance herself from him the moment God told her to, she ends up with a testimony that does not mirror the prophetic words she'd received. Henry ends his relationship with her three months later and leaves the church. Had she done what God told her, Henry would have gotten the deliverance he needed and the two of them would have been happily married. Hear me—this can and does happen —often! The seeds for your future are often there to be sacrificed, and there are some doors that you won't be able to enter until God decides that you're ready. If you go through the window instead to access what you are designated to eventually inherit, you will squander, pervert and delay your inheritance. Think about the prophet Joseph. He had a dream, but his immaturity and impatience led him to share that dream with the wrong people.

Genesis 37:5-11: And Joseph dreamed a dream, and he told it his brethren: and they hated him yet the more. And he said unto them, Hear, I pray you, this dream which I have dreamed: For, behold, we were binding sheaves in the field, and, lo, my sheaf arose, and also stood upright; and, behold, your sheaves stood round about, and made obeisance to my sheaf. And his brethren said to him, Shalt thou indeed reign over us? Or shalt thou indeed have dominion over us? And they hated him yet the more for his dreams, and for his words. And he dreamed yet another dream, and told it his brethren, and said, Behold, I have dreamed a dream more; and, behold, the sun and the moon and the eleven stars made obeisance to me. And he told it to his father, and to his brethren: and his father rebuked him, and said unto him, What is this dream that thou hast dreamed? Shall I and thy mother and thy brethren indeed come to bow down ourselves to thee to the earth? And his brethren envied him; but his father observed the saying.

Note: The name "Joseph" means "He will add" in Hebrew. God doesn't just add to us the pleasures of life, but He has to add bitter in order for us to appreciate all that is sweet. He has to allow us to taste bad before we can appreciate all that is good.

DAY

MIDDAY/NOON
12

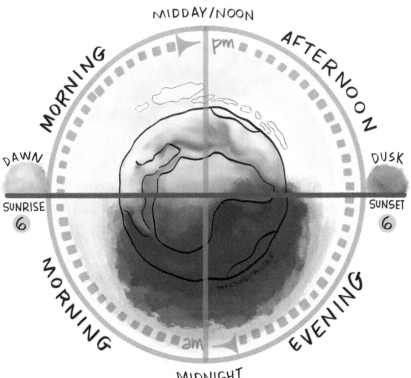

MORNING

AFTERNOON

pm

DAWN

SUNRISE
6

DUSK

SUNSET
6

MORNING

EVENING

am

MIDNIGHT
12

NIGHT

APOSTOLIC
PERIODS

The Dark Days of a Gift

Renown for his unique vocals and mostly for his amazing choreography, Michael Jackson was at the top of his career. He was known on every continent in the world, and he was booked to no ends. He raked in millions of dollars from his albums *Off the Wall, Thriller, Bad, Dangerous and HIStory*, and according to Forbes, he earned 1.1 billion during his adult solo career. His most lucrative years were 1984 when, according to Forbes, he earned $91 million, 1988 when he earned $125 million and 1996 when he earned $71 million. If you were to look at his history of earning, you'd notice that he would have major dips in his earnings from year to year, followed by a sudden surge. I could only imagine what this did to his mental health because a dip signified that people were forgetting about him, rejecting him or moving on without him. Celebrities form relationships with numbers, and not so much with people. This isn't to say that they don't have people around them because they do. It is to say that they learn to associate numbers with their worth and vice versa. But as extreme as some of those dips were, nothing could prepare Michael for the darkest days that he would have to face.

In August of 1993, the Los Angeles Police Department (LAPD) started investigating Michael Jackson after a few claims of child molestation began to surface, and in September of 1993, Michael received his first lawsuit from a family who claimed that the Thriller star had "committed sexual battery against their son." Michael would end up settling this lawsuit, all the while defending his name and character. This created a domino effect with several families emerging, making the same claims against him. And when it was all over with and done, Michael saw a major decrease in his sales, but he would rise again to earn $71 million in 1996. He'd survived his dark days and he was now in the Summer of his gifting once again. People loved him or hated him; either way, he was one of the most celebrated men in the world at that time. But in 2003, he would find himself right back in a season of dark days. He was booked in November of 2003 on child molestation charges, and he was eventually indicted on ten criminal counts, which included, but were not limited to child molestation, abduction, false imprisonment and extortion. In June of 2005, he would be acquitted of all the charges. And while he had been declared innocent, one can only imagine the toll all of this took on his mental health. And please note that I'm not here to indict or exonerate him. I wasn't there, so I don't know what happened. However, my goal is to help you to understand just how dark it can get for a gift.

Like most churches, my church has seen Summer and we've also experienced Winter. There were seasons when it felt like we were at the top and everyone was trying to make their way to Embassy, and then we've experienced seasons when it seemed like everyone was leaving. I've since learned that this is a pattern at most apostolic churches, but knowing this hasn't made it any easier because as a pastor, I'm left to ask myself, "What could I have done differently?" I don't always get the answers to those questions. I've simply learned to let people be humans and to always make sure that I'm looking at the systems of our church to ensure that we are creating space for every gift that walks through our doors. And again, I've learned that we will have great days and we will have dark days. These are the weather patterns of a gift. And hear me—dark days don't always come when we're expecting them. They often sneak up on us the same way a storm sneaks up on an outside wedding.

Like Michael, King David had his great days, followed by the infamous dark days. One day, while working in his father's field, he was called into the house, where he found someone he likely recognized from afar. It was the prophet Samuel. Prophet Samuel was a celebrity to the Jews at that time, and there he was, standing in David's living room! Nevertheless, David composed himself, but that composure was short-lived. All of a sudden, Samuel approached the teenager (he was around 15-years old) and lifted a horn of oil over his head. He then anointed him king of Israel. The Bible says that after this, the Spirit of the Lord came upon David (see 1 Samuel 16:13). This was a great day, and it would be followed by more great days! About two years later, David would find himself being summoned to the palace. Imagine how nervous and excited he was when he learned that the king was personally requesting him to play the harp for him. Three years later, David would find himself, once again, in the king's presence, but this time, in unfavorable conditions. They were on the battlefield, and David had been sent there to deliver food and supplies to his brothers. Nevertheless, the righteous indignation of God had overtaken him, and before long, David found himself in the center of the battlefield, standing over a dead giant. He then took Goliath's sword and decapitated him with it. This was like a valiant moment at a football game. Both teams are tied, and there are only twelve seconds left in the game. The ball finds its way into Ricky, the quarterback's hands, and he begins to run with all of his might. This feat looks impossible, but he's willing to put everything he has into those last few seconds. In this moment, he's more than a football player, he is also a sprinter. He has to be faster and wiser than his opponents. He can hear the commentator screaming as if he's bet on the game, "Five! This kid is a rocket! Four! Three! Two! One! Touchdown!" He made it at the very last moment, and his bravery wins the game. This is likely how David felt as he stood over the giant, and then, subsequently watched as the Philistine army began to flee for their lives. Once again, he'd proven his love and loyalty to the king, and most importantly, to God. This is what it felt like to be on top! Before all of these great victories, David had enjoyed a few private victories, having slayed both a lion and a bear. And now, he was being publicly recognized and celebrated. And if things couldn't get any better, he ends up becoming close friends with the king's son, Jonathan. His future was definitely bright!

David was now a celebrity living in the castle. His rags-to-riches story was being shared both near and afar. But this would all change because light needs darkness to shine its brightest! The start of David's dark days takes place in 1 Samuel 18:5-9, which reads, "And David went out whithersoever Saul sent him, and behaved himself wisely: and Saul set him over the men of war, and he was accepted in the sight of all the people, and also in the sight of Saul's servants. And it came to pass as they came, when David was returned from the slaughter of the Philistine, that the women came out of all cities of Israel, singing and dancing, to meet king Saul, with tabrets, with joy, and with instruments of musick. And the women answered one another as they played, and said, Saul hath slain his thousands, and David his ten thousands. And Saul was very wroth, and the saying displeased him; and he said, They have ascribed unto David ten thousands, and to me they have ascribed but thousands: and what can he have more but the kingdom? And Saul eyed David from that day and forward." David had now come face-to-face with the highest-ranking demon of them all: Envy. This is the prince or principality you will almost always encounter in the wilderness right between the valleys of breakdown and breakthrough! And it was all because a group of women decided to use their beautiful talents to write a song that they probably felt would capture the attention of the handsome young David. What they hadn't realized was that the song would have an adverse effect. Instead of flattering David, their love song marked the beginning of his dark days.

The Bible doesn't tell us whether or not King Saul knew that David had been anointed as the next king, but what we can gather from the text is that, at some point, he realized that he had been hosting and training his replacement the whole time. After this, Saul began to plot against David and this would culminate with David going on the run.

The dark days of a gift include the days of:
- **Infancy:** This is the stage or phase when the gift makes the most mistakes. This is the stage or phase when your gift or talent is beginning to reveal itself, but it has not borne any fruit, nor does it capture the attention of the audience you're called to. This is when a ballerina hurts herself the most, a potter breaks a lot of his inventory and a carpet installer wastes a lot of carpet by cutting it in the wrong way.
- **Imperfection:** This is the stage when the creative's potential can clearly be seen, but his or her skill and abilities are far from excellent. During this phase, creative gifts often sell their services and products for way less than they're worth. This causes them to draw a less-than-favorable clientele. And it is the frustration that they feel that will either push them to the next phase or provoke them to quit altogether.
- **Transition:** By this time, the creative has had it. Frustrated, underpaid and underappreciated, the gift then withdraws himself or herself to a cave. In some cases, the individual will declare that he or she will no longer provide the products or services that he or she had been providing, or the creative will announce that he or she is taking a break. In this, creatives have to

withdraw themselves into their caves seasons so they can reflect and decide if they want to continue in their fields. This also marks the moment when the creative is willing to sacrifice his or her own business or career if something doesn't change. This frustration often leads the individual to establish the rules, policies, guidelines, and boundaries that are needed to protect whatever he or she is building and to protect the builder's mental health.

- **Development:** This is the season when the creative decides that he or she wants to go forward in building, however, the creative realizes that he or she needs help. Creatives then invest time and funds into books, mentorship programs and any other tools of development that they can find.
- **Beginning:** This is the emergence of a gift. This is the hour and time when the creative reemerges with, for example, a better website, contracts, professional branding, and most of all, standards or, better yet, boundaries. This is when the individual has come to recognize the value of what he or she offers.

Consider the days of Noah. Before he began to build the ark, Noah was likely considered just another guy around town, but the moment he started building the ark, people began to ask questions. There's no biblical record of Noah warning the people about the coming flood, but what we do know is that Noah obeyed God and began to build. At first, the people didn't know what he was doing, but as the ark grew in size, they likely began to ask questions. When and if they got an answer, we can safely assume that they thought that Noah was straitjacket worthy. This means that the moment people began to realize that Noah was preparing for a flood, Noah entered his dark days. Can you imagine the laughter, the stares and the cruel jokes he had to endure? Nevertheless, through it all, he had to keep building. And the days would only get darker. When Noah finally entered the ark, he wasn't excited that he and his family were safe. He was thankful, I'm sure, but what people don't realize is that Noah more than likely lost some of his daughters in that flood.

- **Genesis 7:1:** And the LORD said unto Noah, Come thou and all thy house into the ark; for thee have I seen righteous before me in this generation
- **Genesis 7:7:** And Noah went in, and his sons, and his wife, and his sons' wives with him, into the ark, because of the waters of the flood.

To understand this, we have to understand Jewish traditions at that time. Whenever a young woman married, she was considered the property of her husband's family, and by property, I don't mean that she was considered a slave or an object. I mean that she then moved in with her husband's family and she had to abide by their cultures and traditions. A father's sons did not move out of his house; they would just have their own rooms and sides to that house. This is to say that Noah likely had daughters, but they didn't live with him. The commandment he'd received from God was for him to lead all of his household into the ark. Can you imagine the agony he and his wife experienced knowing that they had daughters outside the ark who were about to suffer an unimaginable death? What about the daughter-in-laws that were in the ark? How did they respond, knowing that their fathers, mothers, siblings and the rest of their families were about to drown or were in the middle of drowning? These were the dark days of Noah and his family. For about 150 days, Noah and his crew sat on the ark, knowing that every person and every creature outside that ark was either dead or dying. What would the Earth be like after the flood? How would they survive? Nevertheless, they had to draw their faith from their histories with God. The same is true for us. In our dark days, we have to draw from our histories with God. All the same, these are not seasons when we should embrace self-pity. Instead, we should utilize these moments to mature in character, grow our anointing and perfect our skills. When Michael Jackson found himself in a low place, he didn't quit. Instead, he withdrew himself and came back stronger and better.

We will have moments when we are at the top of our mountains, just as we will have moments when we are in the lowest parts of the valley. Every gift has to learn how to manage each moment, and every gift has to learn the art of self-management. This means that we have to know when we need to withdraw ourselves, when we should speak, when we should remain silent, when we should build, when we should tear down, what doors we should open and what doors we should shut. This is because dark days are inevitable, but they are all a part of the creative's diet. Joseph had plenty of dark days, David had plenty of dark days, Daniel had plenty of dark days, Noah had plenty of dark days, Apostle Paul had plenty of dark days, and the list goes on. The same is true for you and I. And how we manage these days will determine whether we ascend in the industries we're called to or whether we'll descend into madness.

The Dark Hours of a Gift

Again, there are 12 numbers on a clock, and they all represent a slice of the pie that every creative must eat. And before the dawning of that gift, these 12 slices of reality can be rather bitter. These pieces (once again) are:

1. Rejection
2. Self Rejection
3. The Removal of the Speck
4. The Confrontation
5. The Exodus
6. Obscurity
7. Silence
8. Puberty
9. Breakthrough
10. Sacrifice
11. Revelation
12. Emergence

24 HOURS
TWILIGHT
12
NIGHT
12
DAY
DUSK
DAVID
SAUL
APOSTOLIC PERIODS

I want you to imagine standing on the face of a giant clock. Your hour of emergence is at noon, but it is now midnight, so you've just stepped onto the first slice of pie you'll have to eat, which is rejection. Again, each hour represents a season. Right now, I'm about to walk you around that clock so that you can understand each season you have to digest.

12:00 AM: Rejection

Think about the moment Moses confronted the Egyptian man who had been harassing the Hebrew man. Moses hadn't been able to fit in his whole life, and at this moment, he likely thought that standing up for his brethren would finally prove to them that he wasn't the spoiled, entitled brat that they thought he was. He would finally prove that he was on their side, and they would accept him. He killed the Egyptian and he was confident that his secret would be safe with the other Hebrews. It wasn't. Exodus 2:11-14 details this event. It reads, "And it came to pass in those days, when Moses was grown, that he went out unto his brethren, and looked on their burdens: and he spied an Egyptian smiting an Hebrew, one of his brethren. And he looked this way and that way, and when he saw that there was no man, he slew the Egyptian, and hid him in the sand. And when he went out the second day, behold, two men of the Hebrews strove together: and he said to him that did the wrong, Wherefore smitest thou thy fellow? And he said, Who made thee a prince and a judge over us? Intendest thou to kill me, as thou killedst the Egyptian? And Moses feared, and said, Surely this thing is known."

Things weren't going as planned. Instead of being a revered hero and celebrated by his people, Moses realized in that moment that he did not have an ally with his tribe; the same was true regarding his Egyptian connections. Hear me—one of the hardest seasons to endure is the season of rejection. Rejection, within itself, is truly not that hard to overcome once you have a better understanding of it, but when you're in the infancy of your assignment, it can feel unbearable! This is because the human soul is not designed to process or digest rejection! That's like trying to digest plastic! The stomach of a human was not created or equipped to digest plastic!

This is your midnight! This is the startup of your journey. Maybe you are a singer, and you're trying to showcase your gift to a few people, but no one seems to be paying you any attention! Everyone has an opinion about you that does not reflect who you truly are! This is because even in your exposure, God hides you! It is not your time to be glorified! It is not your hour to be recognized! In this moment, you have to eat the rejection until your stomach is strong enough to process it! And by processing it, I mean that you have to extract all of the nutrients from it and discard the waste! This is the hour that most gifts have trouble getting by! This is the hour that most creatives give up, but the ones who overcome this season typically go on to finish the race, because again, this is the hardest season for most gifts!

1:00 AM: Self Rejection

Rejection has a domino effect. Being rejected by others, especially your peers and loved ones, will cause you to question yourself, doubt yourself or maybe even dislike yourself. Some people even learn to hate themselves. Can you imagine how Moses felt the moment his brethren rejected him? Or consider how Joseph felt when he was locked up in prison, having been sold into slavery by his brothers, and then, subsequently harassed and lied on before being tossed into prison. Or think about the moment Elijah went on the run. He was ready to forfeit his assignment and his life, not because he was afraid of what Jezebel planned to do to him, after all, he wanted to take his own life. Elijah felt alone in that moment. The rejection had taken so much of a toll on him that he began to reject himself. This is all suicide is; it's self-rejection. And like the season of rejection, this is a difficult season to endure because you're trying to process all of the events that are happening around you, all the while fighting with your self-image. One of the reasons for this is because, in this hour or season, you truly don't know your identity. Sure, you're Christian. You may be a prophet of God or an apostolic warrior, but this is not the fullness of your identity. It's just your function, and while our functions are one-third of our identities, they don't form the full picture. And when we don't fully understand who we are, this makes it harder for us to know what to do, where to go, who to partner with, who to disconnect from; it can be quite taxing on the soul! But the way to overcome self-rejection and come out of this season unscathed is simply by placing your faith in God. This is the season when you need to study the Word of God more than you've ever studied; this is your season of learning! This is not your season to teach because your soul is trying to process everything you're enduring, but it doesn't have the language, the experience or the understanding needed to properly digest it all! So, if you go live on Facebook, Instagram or YouTube, you'll only complain and whine. Complaints aren't just words; they are the accents of your last season! Spend this time with God so that you can get to know Him better. This will allow you to be prepared when the three o'clock hour hits!

3:00 AM: The Removal of the Speck

This is self-surgery and it's painful! Matthew 7:3-5 reads, "And why beholdest thou the mote that is in thy brother's eye, but considerest not the beam that is in thine own eye? Or how wilt thou say to thy brother, Let me pull out the mote out of thine eye; and, behold, a beam *is* in thine own eye? Thou hypocrite, first cast out the beam out of thine own eye; and then shalt thou see clearly to cast out the mote out of thy brother's eye."

This is the season when you need to be working on yourself, getting all of the therapy and deliverance you'll need to cast all of that junk out of your soul from your previous seasons. This is not the time for you to create a bunch of flyers and start marketing yourself! This is the time when you need to surround yourself with mentors and you need to force yourself to sit still! For example, in this particular season, Moses went to Midian where he sat under the tutelage of his father-in-law, Jethro, for forty years! During this season, he served as a shepherd! He had one of the most unattractive jobs, and that was cleaning up behind sheep! I'm sure that he wanted to return to Egypt. Maybe, he wanted to apologize to Pharaoh, after all, before his fall from glory, he had free reign of the castle, serving as Pharaoh's step-grandson. He had to start a new diet! He would no longer sit at the fancy table of Pharaoh, enjoying all of the Egyptian delicacies and buffets. Instead, he now had to kill his own food. This looked nothing like his former life! He didn't have servants serving him, now he was required to serve! This is the season when he had to confront his entitlement; this was the season when he had to be fully purged of all of the rejection and traumas he'd experienced in Egypt. But before he could go back and be a deliverer, he had to first receive deliverance! And this wouldn't be a one-time event, standing at an altar, coughing up devils! This would be a 40-year journey that would test every ounce of his being! But once he removed the speck from his own eyes, he would be able to see clear enough to help his brethren.

4:00 AM: The Confrontation

Can you imagine the moment when Moses realized that he had to return to Egypt to save his brethren? After being rejected, he'd probably echoed the same sentiments that many of us echo. He likely said to himself, "When I make it in this life, I'm going to treat them how they treated me!" And for forty years, he lived up to this because he wasn't mature enough to understand the rejection! We have to stop expecting bound people to behave civilly! It took Moses forty years to understand this! And finally, the hour came when he realized that he was needed! Those long talks with Jethro and all of those moments when he'd had to fight off wild animals just to save Jethro's sheep were now causing the scales to fall off his eyes! Like most shepherds, he'd likely had that moment when he was fighting off a vicious animal that had one of the sheep in its clinches. Not realizing that he was trying to save it, the sheep had bitten him! Nevertheless, he'd saved the sheep, but of all the wounds he'd gotten in that fight, the sheep's bite had been the most painful one because he had been holding it close when it bit him.

Moses had to return to save the people who'd rejected him! Note: most creatives reject their assignments the moment they say, "They'll need me, and when they do, I won't be there!" This is an agreement; this is a confession, and if you've said this, I challenge you to renounce it! Proverbs 25:21-22 instructs us this way, "If thine enemy be hungry, give him bread to eat; and if he be thirsty, give him water to drink: for thou shalt heap coals of fire upon his head, and the LORD shall reward thee." Who will reward you?! The Lord! We have to stop expecting people to reward us with their acceptance or gratitude, and just allow the Lord to reward us!

The journey from Midian to Egypt is believed to be over 6,600 miles! Some scholars argue that it was closer to 400 miles, but either way, that was a long journey! Moses' assignment had come in. He would have to go and confront the man who once served as his grandfather. This is the season when we have to confront our own demons. This is the season when we have to ring hell's doorbell and put the entire host of hell on notice that we have said yes to our assignments, whether those assignments be ministerial or non-ministerial. Remember, our purpose is to destroy the works of the enemy, but our calling is the way by which we accomplish this! Sure, we've gone through our own personal deliverances at this time, but it's time to confront the strongman through an event called intercession! This is when we take everything we've learned and put it to use! This is also the moment when we have to return to our brethren and prophesy deliverance to them. After this, we have to show them our wounds, testify about our freedom and our God, and help to build their faith; this way, they'll be preparing themselves for deliverance while we are confronting Pharaoh on their behalves!

5:00 AM: The Exodus

We often think that this is the hour of glory, but it's actually the beginning of the wilderness journey. You've confronted Pharaoh and amassed a few followers, and now, it's time for you to leave Egypt behind once again, but here's the caveat —you're leaving Egypt permanently! One of the lessons I've learned over the course of my life is that many people have no problem leaving Egypt, just as long as the door is open for them to return. This is because most people don't initially take deliverance seriously. It's just something they are willing to try out in hopes that it'll make life easier for them, but when they realize that they actually have to change their minds and their lifestyles, most of those same people will turn around and head back to Egypt. In truth, most folks don't want freedom, they just want life to be easier. Howbeit, in this hour and season, you aren't just helping others to get free, you are permanently disassociating yourself from your past; you are burning the bridge between your past and your future. You're at the point of no-return and you're bringing a few people with you, whether it be your family or a group of social media followers. This is the time when it feels like all hell has broken loose and is now trying to assassinate you. In this season, you'll want to give up, but what will keep you from throwing in the towel will be the faces of the people who are looking up to you and depending on you for their own freedom, even if those people are your children.

Please note that it is easy to confuse this moment with your hour of emergence in whatever industry you're called to, but it's far from that! This is the start of the longest season of your life, and again, that is the wilderness season.

Nestled between Egypt (sin) and the Promised Land are three obstacles that you'll have to face. They are your past, the Red Sea and the wilderness. Behind you, you'll find your past quickly approaching, hoping to capture you and keep you from moving on without it. In front of you, you will find your personal Red Sea. This is the blood or the sacrifices you will have to make in order to even qualify for your Promised Land. And truth be told, there is a moment in that space of time when you will wonder if you can somehow marry your Egypt with your Promised Land. But the sound of your past gaining up on you will serve as a reminder to you that you don't have too much time to make a decision. Like many creatives, you may try to marry the two worlds or systems together, and if this happens, you will stall your deliverance. Instead, you will find yourself back in the custody of your Pharaoh, and this time, he will place more taskmasters around you and make your load heavier! "When the unclean spirit is gone out of a man, he walketh through dry places, seeking rest, and findeth none. Then he saith, I will return into my house from whence I came out; and when he is come, he findeth it empty, swept, and garnished. Then goeth he, and taketh with himself seven other spirits more wicked than himself, and they enter in and dwell there: and the last state of that man is worse than the first" (Matthew 12:43-45).

However, if you pass through the Red Sea, you will be walking away from jobs, relationships and realities that you've grown familiar with, and you will be shutting these doors permanently! All the same, the people who are following your lead who have also made major sacrifices for this journey will hinge all of their hopes upon you. Nevertheless, this deliverance signals a permanent change in your life and in the lives of those closest to you. It denotes the beginning of your emergence, but get this—we're dealing with a spectrum—the beginning of a gift's emergence always starts with obscurity!

6:00 AM: Obscurity

Now, you've entered the wilderness. The sights are different, the smells are different and the sounds are different. Every comfort you once enjoyed is long gone! If you've brought anyone with you who God told you to leave behind, you will enter a sub-season called Strife. Can two walk together unless they are in agreement? Sure, you may agree on somethings, but Lot doesn't have the same commitments, convictions or assignments as you, so he's going to challenge your every decision. And your personal Lot can be a boyfriend, a girlfriend, a best friend or anyone from your past. And once you get rid of Lot, you will then find yourself feeling alone, even though you may have many followers. Get this—Abram had followers, but no one was on his level. Everyone who followed him out of Ur was a servant. And don't get me wrong, they are people too, and I'm sure that Abram had many conversations with them, just as he did with his wife, Sarah. But none of them had heard from God; they didn't fully understand or agree with Abram's decision to leave his family behind to follow a God he could not see. So, while Abram was surrounded by people, he likely felt lonely. This is why many gifts feel lonely, even in crowded spaces. It's not that you're alone, the problem is, you may outrank everyone in the room. That's like being a college professor in a room filled with four-year old children. Yes, they're smart and they all have potential, but they are many seasons behind you, so you don't have like interests. As a matter of fact, this is the season when you feel like you're helping everyone, but you have no one to turn to for help. This is when you find yourself being the proverbial "strong friend." All the same, you've been on a platform; you've led many people towards freedom, but no one seems to know or respect you. You're anointed and you can hear the voice of God, but the people around you can't seem to hear or respect your voice. Maybe, you started a church in this season, and you've watched the people you once helped walk out of your church one after the other. Or maybe, you started building your bakery business, but no one is supporting you. Everyone seems to either want a freebie or a discount. You've helped others to launch their businesses, but the majority of them prove to be entitled and ungrateful. This is similar to the hour when Jesus healed the ten lepers, but only one came back to show his gratitude. It is during this time that you'll have to intentionally and strategically withdraw yourself from the people around you. And you have to make sure that you're accountable to someone. Most importantly, it is necessary for you to fight off the urge to go into isolation. There will be times and moments when you will want to escape it all and just hit the reset button on life, but you can't. All the same, this is not the time to go live and tell the world where you are because even though you've overcome Pharaoh, there are other enemies around that do not want to see you reach your Promised Land. And hear me

—in this season, you'll want more than anything to tell the world about what you've gone through, what you're going through and you may even want to share every prophetic word that you've received. If you want to know the psychology behind this mindset, it's simple—subconsciously, you are trying to gather an audience to explain not only what you've just gone through, but to validate and affirm who you are. But if you do this, you'll end up getting the attention of witches and warlocks. These people feed on desperate gifts who are in their six o'clock hours. This is because the light of day hasn't yet arrived to put darkness in its place. And these witches and warlocks disguise themselves as Christians. Many of them disguise themselves as prophets and prophetesses, and they will happily prophesy to you. What's both confusing and amazing about this is, they can be accurate with some of their prophetic utterances! And if you get entangled with one of these people, you will be in the clutches of Jezebel, and Jezebel will stop at nothing to destroy you. The point is, surround yourself with wise counsel. Proverbs 11:14 says it this way, "Where no counsel is, the people fall: but in the multitude of counselors there is safety." And as a reminder, don't attempt to expose yourself in this season. It's not your moment to be seen or celebrated. This is why every creative needs a pastor. You need someone to tell you to sit down, even though you may not necessarily want to hear this at that time. But it's for your safety and to ensure that everyone who is following your lead doesn't find themselves in a pit. "Let them alone: they be blind leaders of the blind. And if the blind lead the blind, both shall fall into the ditch" (Matthew 15:14).

Lastly, this is your cave season. You will need to systematically remove yourself from all of the distractions around you so that you can hear from God. Just remember to be accountable with your leaders so that you are not tempted or brought back into bondage by a devil disguising itself as an angel of light.

7:00 AM: Silence

It's the break of day, and everyone around you seems to be murmuring and complaining. All the same, you have not yet reached your Promised Land. What was supposed to be a short journey has now proved itself to be everything but that. You thought you'd be married by now! You thought you'd be out of poverty by now! You thought you'd be further than you are by now! And the voices around you don't make this easier! They've placed all of their hope in you, and you're now proving yourself to be—human! Of course, God wants you to return His glory to Him so that they can place their hope and faith in Him, but all eyes seem to be fixated on you and your choices. People are falling away, walking away and slandering your name. And to add insult to injury, the manna God is giving you comes in one flavor: bland! So, you start to remember all of the delicacies you once ate in Egypt. And it's as if hell can hear your thoughts. The voice of Pharaoh seems to resurrect itself in your conscious, and he sounds like he's sorry for everything he's done! You're being tempted to return to Egypt in your mind, and the people around you are tempting you to return to your Egyptian ways! This is still a part of your season of obscurity. This is when you need to pull yourself away from all that is familiar and pray, pray and pray some more! And you have to add an extra layer of consecration to your diet; you need to fast until you no longer look like the "you" everyone knows!

I've seen more gifts quit in this hour than in any other hour because nothing seems to be agreeing with them, and it makes more sense logically to return to that old job, that former lover or that toxic family. You're praying, but God doesn't seem to want to acknowledge anything that you are saying. This is because the Teacher is quietest during the tests! You're at the crossroads of your emergence. The light of day has now revealed your whereabouts, and hell seems to have taken notice. But you're safe. You're just frustrated with it all, and it is during this season when you'll question yourself the most, asking:

- Did I really hear from God?
- Why isn't He speaking back?
- Is God mad at me?
- Did I do something wrong?
- Is one of these people in my circle praying against my success?
- Do I have a witch in my midst?

This is normal! Because, in this season, nothing seems to make sense. You've built the business and you've gotten a few customers, but they aren't the types of clients you want.

You've started sharing your gifts with the world, and it seems that everyone around you wants to discount you. And again, the hardest part of this season is the silence of God. You may feel rejected by God, but don't do what King Saul did when he wasn't hearing from God. He consulted with a witch! 1 Samuel 28:3-7 reads, "Now Samuel was dead, and all Israel had lamented him, and buried him in Ramah, even in his own city. And Saul had put away those that had familiar spirits, and the wizards, out of the land. And the Philistines gathered themselves together, and came and pitched in Shunem: and Saul gathered all Israel together, and they pitched in Gilboa. And when Saul saw the host of the Philistines, he was afraid, and his heart greatly trembled. And when Saul inquired of the LORD, the LORD answered him not, neither by dreams, nor by Urim, nor by prophets. Then said Saul unto his servants, Seek me a woman that hath a familiar spirit, that I may go to her, and inquire of her. And his servants said to him, Behold, there is a woman that hath a familiar spirit at Endor."

As you can see, Saul had done great things by putting away the sorcerers and making sorcery illegal. Of course, we know that God had left Saul by then, but hear me—God is gracious! This is made evident when we read the scriptures! The problem is, Saul didn't have a heart of repentance! He continued to come against God by coming against the prophetic word that had been spoken regarding David. But again, in this season when it feels like God is the most silent, don't seek after any other voice. Just know that God is with you, and be sure to pray, repent and study the Word on a daily basis.

8:00 AM: Puberty

The silence has broken, the prophetic words are coming in and your hope is restored! This is a glorious hour! All the same, your voice has changed; it's gotten deeper and you've gotten wiser! You now have an inkling of an idea as to who you are, what you're called to do and the rank you're called to. At this stage, you think you know everything you need to know to make it to your Promised Land! The people who've survived the journey with you now have a renewed hope and trust in you, and now, you're able to reproduce yourself. But the problem is, many of the prophetic words have yet to come to pass; you still haven't arrived in your Promised Land, even though you can sense it. It feels so close, and yet, so far! This is your season of temptation! You can do it on your own ... or so you think! Why wait on the promise when there are doors in front of you that look promising? In this season, many gifts make the mistake of going through those doors; that is, they leave their churches, they quit their jobs and they walk away from the people they feel are holding them back. They then go and try to make the promise come to pass on their own! And this is when they give birth to Ishmael. Ishmael looks, sounds and feels like a fulfilled prophecy, but at some point, reality will set in and the gift will find himself or herself having to make one of the hardest decisions of his or her adult life; they will have to sacrifice that business, ministry or whatever it is that they've spent years building so that they can go back and follow the steps they attempted to skip.

Thankfully, not all gifts fall into the trap of allowing their hormones (carnality) to dilute their destinies, but many do. In this particular hour, you will feel like you know more than your pastor, more than your mentor, more than your parents, more than your boss, more than whomever it is that is in place serving as your leader. You may have noticed your leader's weaknesses, but hear me and hear me clearly—do NOT attempt to expose your leader or leaders in this hour! Yes, they are humans as well! This was the hour that Ham found himself him. Genesis 9:20-25 reads, "And Noah began to be an husbandman, and he planted a vineyard: And he drank of the wine, and was drunken; and he was uncovered within his tent. And Ham, the father of Canaan, saw the nakedness of his father, and told his two brethren without. And Shem and Japheth took a garment, and laid it upon both their shoulders, and went backward, and covered the nakedness of their father; and their faces were backward, and they saw not their father's nakedness. And Noah awoke from his wine, and knew what his younger son had done unto him. And he said, Cursed be Canaan; a servant of servants shall he be unto his brethren."

Ham was still in puberty, but there's something about testosterone that makes us reveal the conditions of our hearts. In other words, it gives us and others a snapshot of who we're becoming. This isn't the hour to quit or to challenge the leaders in your life. This is the hour when you have to put your flesh on the altar and kill it—again! And you have to be mindful of the people you associate with. As a pastor, I've noticed that people tend to pair up the most in this particular season, and what's worse is, they don't always pair up with the right people! I've watched people form friendships and friend groups, and I've watched those same people slowly but surely disconnect from the church, first mentally and emotionally, and then, physically. This is because they made the mistake of allowing their desires to be seen and heard overwhelm them, and they began to talk to the wrong people! These people then validate them by confirming their suspicions and reflecting their frustrations back to them. In the world of psychology, this is called "mirroring." Mirroring is a strategy that narcissists use to build rapport with the people they are interested in bonding with. They do this by mirroring or pretending to share the same beliefs, likes and dislikes as their potential prey. It is not only designed to create a soul tie between the narcissist and his or her victim, but it's also designed to accelerate this process. I've witnessed this many times, and it almost always looks the same! People find what they think are their spiritual doppelgangers in the church, and they grow so close that they become almost inseparable! But once the narcissist has them fully convinced, they then begin to suggest to them that:

1. They're more anointed than their pastors.
2. Their pastors don't like them, are jealous of them or

are intimidated by them. This is pretty much similar to what Satan did with Eve. He made her believe that God was somehow threatened by her potential. Why else would He tell her not to eat from the Tree of the Knowledge of Good and Evil when, according to the serpent, she'd be like, equal to or as God?!

3. Their pastors don't like them (the undercover or covert narcissists). This is when the narcissist uses the soul tie to seduce or pretty much drag their prey away from the church altogether or away from the church that he or she is called to. They do this by saying, for example, "I think my time is up at the church. God has been dealing with me for a long time and telling me to separate myself." This language suggests to the listener that God is against that particular ministry and is about to judge it. This is designed to get the other party to flee from the church, and again, the benefit of this separation to the gift is that he or she no longer has to follow the steps or submit himself or herself to the rest of the developmental process.

The hour of puberty is challenging, but you can overcome it by simply remaining prayerful and not allowing yourself to be tempted or seduced outside of God's will. All the same, you have to be mindful of who you attach yourself to in this hour because your potential is not only showing, but people can also start seeing the height of that potential, meaning they can see that you're called or anointed to do great things. At the same time, you don't fully know who you are, nor do you truly understand how manipulative and cunning some people are. So, at this stage, you're just trying to be nice and love everyone, not realizing that in this hour or season, you are like a college football player that has captured the attention of scouts both near and far! We all know what happens to many of these guys! They end up taking one DNA test after the other, and some of them end up paying tens of thousands of dollars in child support because, hear me—the minute your potential begins to break ground and bud, every opportunist within one hundred miles of you will take notice! At this stage, you don't have security surrounding you! At this stage, you're not too familiar with "groupies." And yes, they do position themselves in churches, and they set their eyes on the emerging leaders within those churches! Again, they use a wile called mirroring to capture the attention of the creatives in their sights, and once they've gotten their attention, they begin the bonding process.

Just remember that if God said it, it will come to pass! Don't try to rush it and don't abort the process simply because you feel like it's time for you to make headway. The fruit of patience (long-suffering) is what you'll need the most in this hour.

9:00 AM: Breakthrough

Sarai has just given birth to Isaac; in other words, some of the most pronounced prophecies you've received have been fulfilled! You can see the Promised Land just ahead, and it would appear that your struggles are OVER! This is your season of rest! This is your season of affirmation! This is your season of breakthrough! Everyone who once slept on your potential is now woke or, better yet, aware of who you are! Yes, even if they're still pretending to be asleep! Doors are starting to open, and it would appear that you are in the Spring of your gifting.

Take this season to rest and to study, but do NOT get too comfortable! This season can give you a false sense of security! There will be times when you'll feel like you've arrived at your Promised Land and that the storms are now over! But remember that the beginning of Spring also marks the onset of hurricane season! This is the time when two climates clash, with the winds from the South (Egypt) clashing with the winds from the North (the Promised Land). Please rest because you're about to enter another challenging season, and that is the season of sacrifice.

In your hour of breakthrough, you'll realize that you no longer crave Egyptian food. In your hour of breakthrough, you'll realize that you are no longer even remotely attracted to Pharaoh! In your hour of breakthrough, you will have forgiven everyone and you will experience peace on every side. This isn't to say that you won't be challenged, but it is to say that the winds will be so low that they won't move you. Consider the story of King David. He'd defeated Goliath, and the man who had been trying to kill him (Saul) was now dead. He'd grieved Saul, and he was now sitting on the throne of Israel. He was at peace. Everything that he needed and wanted was at his disposal, but there's something lodged in the human psyche that causes us to want what we cannot have, even when we have everything we want. Adam and Eve experienced this in the Garden of Eden. They could eat from every tree in that garden except for the Tree of the Knowledge of Good and Evil. Satan knew that if he could plant the seeds of dissatisfaction in their souls, they would never be satisfied. And now, we have inherited this stronghold! This is why David found himself lusting after one of the few women that he could not have: Bathsheba! Truthfully, this is the season when many gifts make their greatest mistakes. This is when we start hearing about scandals and secrets! The emerging gift has gotten too comfortable, and remember, your gift works best in darkness! This is why you shouldn't get too comfortable. Again, enjoy this season and don't forget to use this season to increase your study time.

10:00 AM: Sacrifice

To understand this season, let's look at some scriptures.

- **Genesis 21:14:** And Abraham rose up early in the morning, and took bread, and a bottle of water, and gave it unto Hagar, putting it on her shoulder, and the child, and sent her away: and she departed, and wandered in the wilderness of Beersheba.
- **Genesis 22:3:** And Abraham rose up early in the morning, and saddled his ass, and took two of his young men with him, and Isaac his son, and clave the wood for the burnt offering, and rose up, and went

unto the place of which God had told him.

- **Exodus 8:20:** And the LORD said unto Moses, Rise up early in the morning, and stand before Pharaoh; lo, he cometh forth to the water; and say unto him, Thus saith the LORD, Let my people go, that they may serve me.
- **Joshua 3:1:** And Joshua rose early in the morning; and they removed from Shittim, and came to Jordan, he and all the children of Israel, and lodged there before they passed over.
- **Judges 7:1:** Then Jerubbaal, who is Gideon, and all the people that were with him, rose up early, and pitched beside the well of Harod: so that the host of the Midianites were on the north side of them, by the hill of Moreh, in the valley.
- **1 Samuel 17:20:** And David rose up early in the morning, and left the sheep with a keeper, and took, and went, as Jesse had commanded him; and he came to the trench, as the host was going forth to the fight, and shouted for the battle.
- **Matthew 27:1:** When the morning was come, all the chief priests and elders of the people took counsel against Jesus to put him to death:
- **John 21:4:** But when the morning was now come, Jesus stood on the shore: but the disciples knew not that it was Jesus.

What does all of the aforementioned scriptures have in common? They all mention the morning! There are three times of the day; they are: morning, noon and evening. In John 9:4, Jesus said, "I must work the works of him that sent me, while it is day: the night cometh, when no man can work." The morning is a time of sacrifice. Who wants to get up early in the morning and work?! Most of us want to sleep in until the early or late afternoon, but in this particular hour, your job is to tame your flesh all the more, and this is a full-time job!

In this season, you have the promise, but God just might ask you to return it to Him. This is when you are required to sacrifice Isaac! You've sent Ishmael away and you've overcome many obstacles, but of all the sacrifices you've made, this one seems to be the hardest. The purpose of this particular sacrifice is to keep your heart from idolizing the promise. This is the season when it may feel as if God cannot be satisfied. I mention this because many creatives find themselves becoming angry with God in this season, and this anger oftentimes manifests as them praying less, pulling away from the church or it may manifest as rebellion. You've come too far to give up now! Every great season is preceded by an altar, and while this is the biggest sacrifice you've ever been required to make, please note that God is just testing you! This doesn't mean that you won't personally have to sacrifice what you don't want to sacrifice, but it is to say that God will restore to you everything that you've lost and everything that you've sacrificed. Then again, He may stop you just before you shut that door, end that relationship or quit that job! He will provide you with the sacrifice! Just don't eat it!

11:00 AM: Revelation

Oh, the hour of revelation! The most difficult and least understood hour there is! Most gifts never arrive at this season because they are taken out somewhere between 12 am (Genesis) and 11 pm (Jude)! If you thought your exodus was difficult, if you thought the wilderness season was arduous and if you thought your season of sacrifice was unbearable, you haven't seen anything yet! This is the season when Miriam and Aaron will form an alliance against you! This is the season when Judas will betray you with a kiss! This is when you'll come to understand just how cruel envy is!

What if I told you that Joseph and Daniel had similar stories, but Daniel's dilemma was far more taxing! They both faced jealousy, but Daniel experienced something far more sinister; he experienced Envy!

Unlike Daniel, Joseph shared his dreams with the wrong people at the wrong time. This caused him to endure a lot of unnecessary warfare. The next header you'll find after the text talking about Joseph sharing his dreams is, "Joseph Sold by His Brothers." Another way to look at this is, Joseph shared a prophetic word with the wrong people and this caused him to be taken into bondage. In other words, the enemy will stop at nothing to take you back to Egypt! This is what happened to Joseph. It wasn't his hour to be glorified.

He was still immature; he was still in the middle of his process, but the place that he was being processed in could no longer host him. The reason for this is because his brothers' envy had begun to consume them to the point where they wanted him dead. Every creative who presses toward the high mark of their assignment will endure this at some point in their journeys, and to be truthful, this is the highest level of warfare! Think about Jesus. When Herod began to seek after His young life, God instructed Joseph in a dream to take his family and flee to Egypt. Think about one of the scenarios in Jesus' adult life. John 7:1 details this moment. "After these things Jesus walked in Galilee: for he would not walk in Jewry, because the Jews sought to kill him." Why did the Jews want Him dead? Jealousy! The Bible tells us that jealousy is as cruel as the grave (see Song of Solomon 8:6). But hear me—it's a part of the creative's diet. And who do you think jealousy is cruelest to: the person who is being hated on or the person who is the hater? The answer is both, but it would depend on the hated person's proximity to the people who envied him or her! Envy deteriorates the mental health of the person hosting it the most because, in order to use that individual, it must repeatedly torment them with thoughts of the other person, and it must diminish their own accomplishments, self-worth and their perception of themselves. This is cruel! Then again, the person on the receiving end has to master avoiding its darts. How do you think David avoided being pierced by Saul's javelin on three separate occasions?!

In this season, you won't just be experiencing low-level haters. This is when your eyes will open, and you will witness the people that rank alongside you or higher trying to sabotage and blackball you. This is when your alarm is set to go off, even though you thought you were already woke! It is crucial that you don't allow yourself to become bitter in this hour because this is the moment when God begins to reveal the hearts of the people you once looked up to! Your assignment is to not become like them! Your assignment is to intercede for them! But this isn't easy, after all, your heart may be broken because of what you're witnessing! This is when God begins to trust you with His emotions, which means that you will need to stay on your face more, you will need to fast more and you will need to utilize your multitude of counselors all the more! But fret not! This is the eve of your emergence! God didn't allow you to endure all you've endured just to break you. He was creating a leader who wouldn't climax at every Red Sea moment, a leader who wouldn't park in the wilderness and call it quits, a leader who wouldn't get to the Promised Land and then toss Him away! If you survive this season, you can survive anything, and you won't just be a threat to the kingdom of darkness, but you'll become a credible threat! This is when you're not just performing signs, miracles and wonders, but you have become a sign, a miracle and a wonder!

12:00 PM: Emergence

You look around, and the majority of the people who started

off with you have fallen in the wilderness. You are now surrounded by a bunch of new faces and your name has reached the four corners of the Earth. People now know about your skill, your gift or whatever it is that you've mastered.

This is when we start hearing about the Kathryn Kuhlmans, the Nelson Mandelas and the Tyler Perrys. This is when your name supersedes you, and no force on Earth or in hell can erase your name or what you've accomplished. This is also the season when you have created systems that would allow for you to not only reproduce yourself, but to mass reproduce yourself. Genesis 22:17 reads, "That in blessing I will bless thee, and in multiplying I will multiply thy seed as the stars of the heaven, and as the sand which *is* upon the sea shore; and thy seed shall possess the gate of his enemies." This is the season when that word comes to pass, and it doesn't just materialize, but it continues to produce fruit generation after generation. Abraham's name is great, not just in Christianity, but in other faiths as well.

You've done well! Most creatives don't see the dawn of this season, because they don't understand where they are at any given moment. This is why I wanted to give language to every season and help you to understand that what you're facing, what you've gone through and what you will go through are all completely normal! It's not an easy journey for sure. The author of Ecclesiastes (unknown) wrote, "I returned, and saw under the sun, that the race *is* not to the swift, nor the battle to the strong, neither yet bread to the wise, nor yet riches to men of understanding, nor yet favour to men of skill; but time and chance happeneth to them all" (Ecclesiastes 9:11). In other words, every man, both great and small, has a destiny, but that destiny requires a specific diet! A body builder and a Sumo wrestler don't have the same diet or the same exercise regime. Both men are strong and both men have to acquire a certain type and degree of discipline, but they are called to different worlds.

After walking around this clock, the question you have to ask yourself is, "What hour am I in?" You have to be able to locate yourself if you want to finish on time and maintain a sound mind as you pass through each season.

"Show me someone who has done something worthwhile, and I'll show you someone who has overcome adversity."
~Lou Holtz

"There are uses to adversity, and they don't reveal themselves until tested. Whether it's serious illness, financial hardship, or the simple constraint of parents who speak limited English, difficulty can tap unexpected strengths."
~Sonia Sotomayor

Ten Modern Day and Historical Gifts Who've Overcome Adversity

Below, you will find a chart listing some modern day and historical people who've overcome adversity.

Name	Adversity
Bill Gates Founder of Microsoft	Like him or dislike him, Bill Gates is still one of the most successful men in the world. His first company Traf-O-Data failed miserably!
Albert Einstein Physicist	Didn't speak until he was three-years old.
Oprah Winfrey Actress, Talk Show Host	Born in poverty to a single mother in Mississippi. Overcame rape, molestation and the death of her infant son.
Thomas Edison Inventor/ Entrepreneur	Failed more than one thousand times before successfully creating the light bulb!
Will Smith Actor/Rapper	Diagnosed with ADHD as an adult and dyslexia as a child.
Jennifer Hudson Singer/Actress	Had to grieve and overcome the death of her mother, brother and nephew after her brother-in-law shot and killed them in a fit of rage.
Benjamin Franklin Writer, Scientist, Inventor, Diplomat	Dropped out of school at the age of ten because his parents could not afford to continue paying for his education. Went on to become one of America's founding fathers.
Maya Angelou Poet/Civil Rights Activist	Raped by her mother's boyfriend who would later be found murdered. Maya blamed herself for his death, so she stopped talking for five years as a child.

The Times of a Gift

Eternity	Past	Present	Future	Eternity

The purpose of the above spectrum is to help you to get a visual of what time looks like in a vacuum or, better yet, a confined space. Time is temporary, and everything outside of it is eternal.

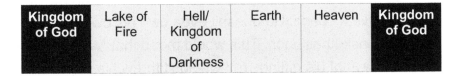

Kingdom of God	Lake of Fire	Hell/ Kingdom of Darkness	Earth	Heaven	Kingdom of God

- **Revelation 20:10:** And the devil that deceived them was cast into the lake of fire and brimstone, where the beast and the false prophet are, and shall be tormented day and night for ever and ever.
- **Revelation 20:14:** And death and hell were cast into the lake of fire. This is the second death.
- **Revelation 21:1:** And I saw a new heaven and a new earth: for the first heaven and the first earth were passed away; and there was no more sea.

The purpose of the aforementioned scriptures isn't to start an eschatological discussion; it is more of a discussion about horology (the study of time). The hosts of the Kingdom of Darkness will be cast into the lake of fire, along with death and hell. But darkness won't be cast into the fire because, logically speaking, darkness doesn't "exist." Sure, we can see it, and it is real, but it doesn't have matter. Again, as we discussed earlier, it simply means the absence of light. God is light. So any dark space can be redeemed or illuminated by light. Darkness simply means void. It represents unrealized potential. For example, let's say that there was a young man named Malachi who was 6 feet, 4 inches tall. On top of this, Malachi loves to play basketball; he's actually really good at it. Some would even argue that he's better than Michael Jordan. But outside of street basketball, Malachi has never witnessed the fullness of his potential. He doesn't have a coach. He doesn't even own his own personal basketball hoop. This would mean that Malachi is in the dark days of his gifting. You wouldn't throw his potential away just because it hasn't been actualized, you'd try to find a way to get Malachi in front of the right people. That's all darkness is; it is a space that has not been filled. It is a space that is void of light, but that does not mean that it is void of potential. What did YAHWEH do after creating the Earth? Let's look at Genesis 2:1 again. It reads, "And the earth was without form, and void; and darkness *was* upon the face of the deep. And the Spirit of God moved upon the face of the waters." This means that God saw nothing but a blank canvas! But get this—there is no end to God's potential, so darkness will always exist! I know that this sounds heretic, but the truth is, Satan and his angels hide in the darkness because they cannot stand in the presence of God. This is why Satan made darkness his kingdom. Think of it this way. You buy a home in the middle of Vegas, and after you get the keys to the house, you find sleeping bags and food debris in one of your rooms. This means that squatters are living in your home! Would you set that entire room on fire? No, you wouldn't. You own that space; it has potential. What you would do is cast out the squatters, clean up the room and fill the room with furniture, pictures and electronic devices, right?! After that, you'd inhabit the room! That room represents a void; it represents potential, but if you clean it up, you can make it into something functional and beautiful. According to West Texas A&M University's website, "Darkness travels at the speed of light. More accurately, darkness does not exist by itself as a unique physical entity, but is simply the absence of light. Any time you block out most of the light – for instance, by cupping your hands together – you get darkness" (WTAMU.edu/What is the Speed of Dark?). In other words, darkness does not exist, meaning it does not live or have mass; it is simply the absence of light.

God's Kingdom is eternal; this means His dominion, His will and His sovereign rule. However, we are eternal creatures trapped within the vacuum of time, and we all have assignments. There is something I'm supposed to accomplish, and there is something that you're supposed to accomplish. We are not just here to take up space. God gave us gifts so that we could become gifts, and ultimately, give Him our gifts. Our goal is to lift Him up through our giftings, and He said that whenever He is lifted up, He will draw all men unto Him (see John 12:32). This is what delights His heart! To be glorified! When God is glorified, people get saved! When God is glorified, people get delivered! When God is glorified, people get healed! And there are many ways that He's glorified. One of those ways is when we place Him first (see Matthew 6:33), repent and seek Him diligently (see Psalm 27:8) and when we use our gifts to glorify Him (see Matthew 25). But we only have a small window of time to accomplish our assignments because we are eternal creatures in a race against time! Even within the confines of time, we have a limited amount of time to build whatever it is that we are set to build! Again, Jesus said, "I must work the works of him that sent me, while it is day: the night cometh, when no man can work," acknowledging that He was living within the constructs of time, meaning He didn't have forever to accomplish His assignment. He had the window of time that God had given Him, and He had to do what He had been sent here to do within that space. The point is, you don't have forever to start that business, write that book, launch that invention or go back to school! Procrastination is the assumption that time will wait for you. Time and chance will happen to all of us, but they won't wait for any of us!

Every gift has a time, a moment or a space given to him or her to build. Sadly enough, most creatives miss their moments because they thought they had more time to learn or master their trades. We all know the phrase, "the wrong place at the wrong time," and while we've rehearsed this phrase time and time again whenever someone, by chance, walked into a bad situation, we must also understand that the will of God is an actual place and space! For example, Shawn gets a call in the middle of the night from one of his friends. He's intoxicated, and he needs a ride home from the club. Shawn's friend is outside the will of God, not because he's at a nightclub, but because he's chosen a lifestyle that is contrary to the lifestyle God has designed him to have. And if he's outside the will of God, Shawn is also outside of God's will (to some degree) because the only way the two of them can walk together is if there is some level of relativity present, meaning they are alike in one area of their lives or more. Shawn's friend, Marcus, asks him to pick him up, noting that he's just gotten into a drunken brawl with another guy. Shawn climbs out of his bed and leaves his house. This is his place of safety; this is his sanctuary. He heads over to the club where Marcus is at to pick him up. But the pickup doesn't go as planned. When Shawn pulls into the parking lot, he sees Marcus from afar arguing with another intoxicated man. All of a sudden, the other guy pulls a gun and starts shooting. One of those bullets makes its way into Shawn's car, killing him instantly. Is this a sad story? Yes, but it happens more often than we think. Marcus is an angry man, and Proverbs 22:24-25 warned us this way, "Make no friendship with an angry man; and with a furious man thou shalt not go: Lest thou learn his ways, and get a snare to thy soul." By being friends with Marcus, Shawn was outside of God's will. Does this mean that he's hell-bound? No. Absolutely not. It means that he was pulled or seduced out of his place of safety by someone who'd chosen an ungodly lifestyle. And I can't emphasize this enough. I'm not saying that we can't minister to people like Marcus, because we can and we should. Friendship deals with proximity to the heart! And being "at the wrong place at the wrong time" doesn't always end in a creative losing his or her life, it could simply mean that the creative is, for example, somewhere playing a video game when he should have been at basketball practice. It could mean that the creative is at home on the phone with her best friend, listening to her talk about a boy she shouldn't have been dating when that creative could have and should have been somewhere building her skill-set. There are distractions all around us, and they are designed to get us outside the will of God, because it is there that Satan can consume this. He goes about as a roaring lion seeking who he can destroy because he doesn't have the legal right to attack everybody at any given time. Who is he looking for? People on the outskirts of God's will because God's will is a carved out space that has walls and limitations! There is a time for you to train or develop your gift, just as there is a time for you to showcase your gift. But if you skip a step, meaning if you don't submit to the season of development, you won't qualify for the season of emergence. Why? Because your potential would still be in its dark phases (infancy); it would still be void because you haven't moved upon it yet. And at some point, you may be too old, too fragile or too tired to do whatever it is that you should be doing right now. Women understand that they have a window of time to have children. After menopause, this window closes. You won't find too many men in the NFL after the age of 40, and most athletes are drafted when they are around 20. In other words, there is a window of opportunity for anyone looking to play for the National Football League. If a young man waits too late, he could miss his moment.

Satan knows that his time is short, so he'll stop at nothing to distract and delay us. This is why we need the fruit of long-suffering.

Patience is Key

It is believed and suggested by some Jews and some theologians that Jesse, David's father, did not believe that David was his biological son. The story goes like this: Boaz married Ruth. Of course, Ruth was not a Jewish woman. Jewish law forbade Hebrew women from marrying Moabite men, but the law did not explicitly forbid Hebrew men from marrying Moabite women. Jewish tradition says that on the night Boaz married Ruth, he'd died, but not before having relations with his new bride. His death was believed to be a punishment from YAHWEH because Boaz had disobeyed the law. And even though Ruth had one sexual encounter with her new husband, she became pregnant that night with their son, Obed. Consequently, Obed was considered illegitimate by the Jews. The same would be true for his son, Jesse, because he wouldn't be a "pure" Jew. Nevertheless, Jesse would go on to become versed in the Talmud and he would become a man of great wisdom and rank. As his name grew, the more Jesse would begin to question his legitimacy, so much so that he'd decided to put away his fully Jewish wife, Nizbeth, because he believed that he was doing her a disservice by being married to her since she was fully Jewish. Again, his grandmother, Ruth, had been a Moabite. Howbeit, by this time, he'd already had seven sons with his wife. Wanting a pure and legitimate son and heir for himself, according to Jewish tradition, Jesse decided to sleep with his wife's Canaanite maidservant because the Jewish law permitted him to intermarry with a Canaanite if that Canaanite had converted to Judaism. The maidservant was definitely qualified. His son from that woman would be considered a legitimate heir. However, the maidservant is said to have truly loved her mistress, Nizbeth, and wanted no part of Jesse's plan. So, she and Nizbeth conspired to make a switch. On the night that he was supposed to sleep with the Canaanite woman, he'd likely had too much to drink. When he'd gone into the room, he hadn't realized that the women had switched up and he was lying with his wife, Nizbeth.

Nizbeth would become pregnant, but she did not tell her husband what she and her maidservant had done. Consequently, Jesse believed that David was another man's son. According to Jewish law, this would mean that Nizbeth would have to be stoned to death, but Jesse still loved Nizbeth, so he never reported the incident. Instead, he decided to raise David as if he were his own, even though he and his other sons with Nizbeth despised David. Many Jews and theologians believe that this is why when Samuel came to visit Jesse and crown one of his sons king, all of the young men were in the house except for David. David was in the field tending to the sheep. Again, this is not scriptural, but it does explain a lot of what we know about David and Jesse's relationship.

1 Samuel 16:2-13: And the LORD said, Take an heifer with thee, and say, I am come to sacrifice to the LORD. And call Jesse to the sacrifice, and I will shew thee what thou shalt do: and thou shalt anoint unto me him whom I name unto thee. And it came to pass, when they were come, that he looked on Eliab, and said, Surely the LORD'S anointed is before him. But the LORD said unto Samuel, Look not on his countenance, or on the height of his stature; because I have refused him: for the LORD seeth not as man seeth; for man looketh on the outward appearance, but the LORD looketh on the heart. Then Jesse called Abinadab, and made him pass before Samuel. And he said, Neither hath the LORD chosen this. Then Jesse made Shammah to pass by. And he said, Neither hath the LORD chosen this. Again, Jesse made seven of his sons to pass before Samuel. And Samuel said unto Jesse, The LORD hath not chosen these. And Samuel said unto Jesse, Are here all thy children? And he said, There remaineth yet the youngest, and, behold, he keepeth the sheep. And Samuel said unto Jesse, Send and fetch him: for we will not sit down till he come hither.
And he sent, and brought him in. Now he was ruddy, and withal of a beautiful countenance, and goodly to look to. And

the LORD said, Arise, anoint him: for this is he. Then Samuel took the horn of oil, and anointed him in the midst of his brethren: and the Spirit of the LORD came upon David from that day forward. So Samuel rose up, and went to Ramah.

In the aforementioned story, we see that David had truly been separated from his brethren. Why this is? We can only speculate. Howbeit, did you know that immediately after being anointed as king, David did not reign as king? Instead, he would find himself back in the field tending to his father's sheep. How do we know this? Look at the story of David and Goliath. 1 Samuel 17:12-15 reads, "Now David was the son of that Ephrathite of Bethlehemjudah, whose name was Jesse; and he had eight sons: and the man went among men for an old man in the days of Saul. And the three eldest sons of Jesse went and followed Saul to the battle: and the names of his three sons that went to the battle were Eliab the firstborn, and next unto him Abinadab, and the third Shammah. And David was the youngest: and the three eldest followed Saul. But David went and returned from Saul to feed his father's sheep at Bethlehem."

Jesse would send David to the battlefield to bring bread to his brothers, and it is there that David would see Goliath mocking the Jews. After a few rebukes and inquiries, David would be granted permission by Saul to fight Goliath, and of course, he would go on to defeat Goliath with a sling and a stone. After the war, David would befriend Jonathan, and according to the scriptures, Jonathan would not allow David to return to his father's house. Meaning, from that moment on, David would live in the palace, but hear me—he still did not reign as king! Here he was, anointed by the prophet Samuel, having killed a giant of a man, and he had favor with the king and his son. However, he still did not immediately reign as king. He would have to endure Saul's jealousy and his many attempts to take his life. He would have to survive his season in the wilderness, and he would have to maintain his honor for the dishonorable Saul before he would eventually take his place as king. In other words, patience is the key to success in every industry! David is believed to have been around 15-years old when he was anointed as king over Israel, but he would not sit on the throne until he was 30-years old. That's a 15 year difference! This is because when David was 15, it was not his time! He was gifted, he was skilled and he was anointed, but it was simply NOT HIS TIME!

This is important to emphasize because many gifts are aborted in the wombs of their development because of impatience! It is difficult to contain a gift once he or she realizes that he or she is anointed, especially when the creative reaches puberty! All too often, we pastors have to witness many of our gifted sons and daughters go through the puberty of their purpose, and we have to sit on the sidelines while their perversions molest their purpose! When these two phases reproduce, we see gifts fade away into the darkness because they then have to deal with adult-sized temptations. And if they haven't been fully equipped or they haven't fully presented themselves to be trained, developed and equipped, the temptation will prove to be too much. Satan begins to seduce them in the same manner he'd seduced Eve. He'd convinced Eve that she didn't need God; she could be her own god. Satan does the same with many of God's gifts. He convinces them that they don't need a pastor, and he uses many devices to get these gifts outside the will of God.

Purpose Pits

There are several purpose pits or traps that Satan sets for the creative or for the gifted. They include:

1. **Offense:** According to the scriptures, a brother offended is harder to win than a strong city (see Proverbs 18:19). Offense is a normal part of the creative's diet, but it takes a certain degree of maturity to digest it properly. Most creative gifts sabotage their assignments when they are in the infancy or toddler stages of their development because they end up throwing one of the five tantrums that are associated with sabotage, which are: gossip, slander, procrastination, quitting, and the worst of them all, falling into the trap of dishonor. These are all tantrums that can have lifelong or generational repercussions.

2. **Church Hurt:** In every church, there are unhealed, undelivered and immature people. Yes, sometimes even on the leadership team! Just like the rest of us, these people are sheep, and get this—sheep bite!

Earlier, we discussed, for example, the believers who have been in a particular church since the beginning of its startup. All too often, these individuals see change as a threat to their security, so they oftentimes challenge new faces and old faces that attempt to birth new systems. And this is what causes a lot of what we've come to know as church hurt. Should you leave your church when you're bitten by one of the members or the leaders? No! You'll likely find this behavior in every church that you go to. Instead, one part of a gift's growth and maturity is sensible, respectable confrontation. In other words, be willing to have a conversation with those people and the leadership, and if nothing is done, then pray about your next move. Keep in mind that your gift works best in darkness, so don't be so quick to run away from every unfavorable situation!

3. **Comparison:** So, you've served at your church for years, and you believe that you're on the not-so-fast track to promotion in your church. You've dreamed of the day when you'd be given an opportunity to preach, but this hasn't happened yet, or maybe it hasn't happened as frequently as you thought it would. Howbeit, some new woman or man shows up at the church, and within months or a few years, that person is already tapping into the favor that you've worked for years to acquire. To add insult to injury, that particular individual has never served in the church, or he or she has rarely served! They are taken in under the

pastor's wings while you're left standing there confused, hurt, offended and frustrated. Hear me—it is NEVER wise to compare your journey with that of another gift! What a lot of people don't realize is that some gifts show up when it's their hour, and as a pastor, we can't ignore this! We don't have the legal right to infringe upon their moments! We can't be willing to disobey God in our attempts to honor the man-made system of first-come, first-serve! That's not how the Kingdom works! Some of these gifts have to be processed quickly because they are in the eve of their assignments, meaning what they're called to accomplish doesn't require much time. The point is, don't allow the enemy to tempt you into comparing your journey with someone else's journey. Your time will come when it's your time, and not a moment sooner!

4. **Romantic Distractions:** Talk to any and every pastor who has pastored for more than three years, and you will hear stories upon stories of gifted people who forsook their assignments and inheritances for what they believed to be love. We are created by Love and we are designed to be loved, just as we are designed to love. But again, there is a season for EVERYTHING underneath the sun! The easiest and most effective way to lure gifts away from their assignments is by appealing to their desires to be understood, accepted and loved on an intimate level. Satan knows this, so he seduces gifts away from their

assignments by sending people their way who mirror their own insecurities, their desires to be loved and their plans for the future. The problem with this is, they don't mirror their anointings! So, the gift is distracted and lured outside the will of God! Can God redeem the time? Of course, He can! But here's the thing—the moment God redeems the time is the moment that Satan will send another distraction their way! In other words, they have to pass that test before they can enter into their next seasons! This is why it is important and necessary to prioritize your purpose over your love life!

5. **The Desire to be Normal:** After making a few sacrifices here and there and having to fight one emotional battle after the other, many gifts look at the people they are called to lead, and they see something that they covet: normality! They want the big house with the white picket fence, the attractive spouse, the adorable and intelligent children, the amazing job and a host of devoted people to call friends and family. They want frequent invitations to outings, financial security and a few vacations here and there. And this doesn't seem too far-fetched when the people you are called to serve seem to enjoy these benefits. But you're not normal! This isn't to say that as a gifted person, you won't get to enjoy these perks; this is to say that many gifts don't get to rest and enjoy the things they want to enjoy until they've accepted or even completed their assignments!

Again, there is a time for everything!

Success and Succession

Queen Elizabeth II was crowned queen of England on June 2, 1953 when she was just 27-years old. Today, she is currently 95-years old, meaning she has reigned as queen of Great Britain for nearly 70 years! Her son, Prince Charles, is next in line for the throne, even though as of 2021, he is 72-years old. And while I can't say for sure if he's anxious to get on the throne, I can say (along with the rest of the world) that his succession to king of England has been a very lengthy one. This is what we call (legal) succession. Succession is defined by Oxford Languages this way, "The action or process of inheriting a title, office, property, etc." Remember, the Kingdom of God is a kingdom of order and protocol. Wherever there is no order, there will be disorder or chaos. This is important to note because we are all moving towards something, whether that something is within the will of God or outside of God's will. If we're in His will, we are following a succession. This succession will allow us to reign or occupy the spaces that we are called to occupy. However, if we move too fast or attempt to occupy or rule over spaces that we are not called to, we are setting ourselves up for a hasty fall. Throughout the Bible, we find many stories of both men and women who pretty much rose to reign by killing off the kings and the queens who were currently on the throne. What's more is that in many of these situations, the men and women who stole those thrones were not called to them. Consequently, you'll notice a pattern throughout the Bible, and that pattern is—they did not reign long. Prince Charles will likely someday become King Charles, but his reign would be incredibly short-lived if he went out of his way to take the throne away from his mother. Instead, to maintain his position, he has to have a heart of honor towards his mother. Proper succession leads to success!

What is success? I think we can all agree that it doesn't look the same for everyone. Success is when you accomplish what you've set out to accomplish. Howbeit, there is Godly success, just as there is ungodly success. Proverbs 10:22 reads, "The blessing of the LORD, it maketh rich, and he addeth no sorrow with it." This tells us that there is a blessing that is not of the Lord and it is often trailed by sorrow. This is why we see so many people stab and claw their way to what looks like success, only to be taken down by scandals. Proper succession means order. And while the journey can be taxing and lengthy, if you follow God's lead, it'll all be worth it in the end!

Your Turn

I wish I could tell you that your time is near. I wish I could get you all pumped up and excited about an event that, in truth, may be several years or even decades down the road. But I think the greatest mistake that a creative can make is to be so focused on the peak of the mountain that he or she forgets to enjoy both the journey and the views on every level of that mountain. Please note that everything that we do and everything that we accomplish is not for us, it's to glorify the Most High God (YAHWEH) and it's to blaze a trail for the people who will follow in our footsteps who also have the assignment of bringing glory to God. I may be a pastor, but my assignment isn't to glorify my own name, make my name great or get as many people as possible to follow me. I am designed to win souls for Christ and to raise up other gifts who will win souls for Christ. Those gifts are designed to raise up more gifts who will raise up more gifts, and this will continue until we step outside of time and lock arms with eternity.

"The two most powerful warriors are patience and time."
~Leo Tolstoy, War and Peace

"A man who dares to waste one hour of time has not discovered the value of life."
~Charles Darwin